Teaching Internet Basics

TEACHING INTERNET BASICS

The Can-Do Guide

Joel A. Nichols

 LIBRARIES UNLIMITED

AN IMPRINT OF ABC-CLIO, LLC
Santa Barbara, California • Denver, Colorado • Oxford, England

Library of Congress Cataloging-in-Publication Data

Nichols, Joel A.
   Teaching Internet basics : the can-do guide / Joel A. Nichols.
     pages cm
   Includes bibliographical references and index.
   ISBN 978-1-61069-741-5 (pbk.) — ISBN 978-1-61069-742-2 (ebook)
1. Internet—Study and teaching. 2. Internet literacy—Study and teaching. I. Title.
   ZA4201.N53   2014
   004.67'8071—dc23   2014024060

ISBN: 978-1-61069-741-5
EISBN: 978-1-61069-742-2

18 17 16 15 14   1 2 3 4 5

This book is also available on the World Wide Web as an eBook.
Visit www.abc-clio.com for details.

Libraries Unlimited
An Imprint of ABC-CLIO, LLC

ABC-CLIO, LLC
130 Cremona Drive, P.O. Box 1911
Santa Barbara, California 93116-1911

This book is printed on acid-free paper ∞

Manufactured in the United States of America

Contents

Foreword

I like to dig deep into the statistics surrounding the digital divide.

I sometimes hope that by looking at the numbers, I'll gain some understanding into how people don't know things.

I don't mean this in a strictly epistemological sense, but more in a social sense. I grew up with technology, even back in the 1980s when this was a little unusual. So similar to the myths that we're told about this recent "born digital" generation, I have a hard time remembering a time before I knew what a computer was. I can still mostly remember learning how to type, how to send an email, how to format a document, and how to build a website. I use most of those skills every week. All of them have become part of my professional as well as my personal life. I can't imagine not being able to do these things.

And yet, when I am teaching technology to my neighbors in Central Vermont, I meet people who don't know the difference between a monitor and a computer (not always obvious!), or email and a website (they used to be more different!), or Facebook and a blog (not even sure I could explain that one!). And I think that knowing more about how people don't know these things, understanding what they do know, and how they form new technological understandings from that, might help me help them.

Nichols has written a book that addresses a need in libraries. For many of us, helping patrons with technology, while we may have only slightly more understanding of it than they do, is a challenging task.

And for patrons who may be coming to technology later in life—whether they are people who didn't learn about computers in school, who are learning disabled, who are from other countries, or who just never got around to it—teaching technology isn't just about the technology. It can also be about mastering fear, or hand-eye coordination, or step-by-step processes, or just venturing into the unknown. So it's not just like learning to ride a bike where there's basically a set of steps and you practice until you get it right. Though that helps.

What Nichols has created are class examples that educators can use that include vocabulary, pre-class set-up information, simple class outlines, and actual projects that students can do within an allotted period of time. Lessons are explained clearly and Nichols takes the time to not just outline the concepts (to teachers who will be explaining them in classes) but offer some accessible explanations of what could go wrong and, best of all, what to do about it if it does.

The most useful parts of this book are simple scripts that can be used to break down even simple concepts into metaphors that students will be able to grasp. Concepts like "What is a login?" and "How do I choose a password?" are addressed in nonthreatening and nonjargony ways that will work well in a library instruction environment. I think many educators will look at these lesson plans and think "This is what I have been looking for!"

There are many complex and interrelated factors that have created the digital divide and it certainly won't be solved with another website, or maybe even with another book. This book is an earnest, straightforward, and well put together collection of things that will help move the ball down the field. The digital divide may never truly be eradicated, at least not in the short term, but with tools like these, we can hope to lessen its effects for both our patrons and our staff.

Jessamyn West
Vermont

Introduction

WHY THIS BOOK?

Digital-literacy instruction is one of the major job duties of 21st-century librarians, whether we like it or not. Patrons who have never touched a computer before come to librarians to ask for help accessing a web page to pay a bill. Teenagers who seem savvy on smartphones end up at a reference desk trying to figure out how to attach their resume in .rtf format. And we are even called on by more advanced users to help with any number of specific tasks: how do I center this picture on a PowerPoint slide? How can I change the name of my Twitter account or revise the security settings on my Tumblr? With no end in sight to what problems library users might have accessing the Internet, librarians need a hands-on and practical guide to approaching—and solving—these digital-literacy instructional challenges. This manual is meant for the librarian who only reluctantly or with some difficulty is teaching computer and Internet basics to patrons with little or no experience. For them, it is a packaged solution with ready-made training scripts and practical examples. It can also be used as a reference for one-on-one coaching situations, where the librarian helps a patron with a specific problem. For more advanced practitioners, this guide will serve as a compendium of basic digital-literacy techniques and approaches. Most librarians will find themselves in between these poles, and this manual gets them up to speed with the latest digital-information needs of users, fills gaps in their own knowledge and experience, and provides a solid and ready-made curriculum to start providing this instruction. Little of this content—and few of these problems—existed when many of us were training in library school, and this cutting edge guide is intended to help.

WHAT ARE THE INTERNET AND
DIGITAL INFORMATION?

The Internet. The World Wide Web. The information superhighway. The cloud. All of these names all refer to different aspects of the same thing: a vast network of interconnected computers all over the world. They are connected by telecommunications lines: phone lines, fiber optic cables, satellite links, cables, and other wired and wireless methods. Being connected means that they can share information electronically. The information shared online is translated into computer language, and then can be sent or accessed anywhere in the world. (Or even in orbit! The International Space Station is also online.)

Digital information is a vague term that can cover anything you access online. It could be any text, photograph, video clip, music file, software programs, data sets, and so on. It refers to anything from banking data to actual online currencies you can use to pay bills. It is necessarily broad. Don't worry about understanding or conveying every example of what digital information is to library customers—most of them already have a general idea, as you do.

The Internet is made up of millions of computers that can talk to each other. And what you can see of the Internet are called web pages. Think of them as the mirror or window that lets us humans understand that computer code. Web pages are the way the Internet gets translated into formats that are understandable to people: into text, into sound, into still or moving image, and so on.

People use the Internet for everything. From dating to banking, applying for jobs, or checking railway schedules around the world, you can now do it all online. Even if you had no Internet experience, just by listening to commercials on TV and the radio, or your neighbors, or a bus full of teenagers, you would know at least that much: you can get that online. But what does that mean?

Remember that the Internet is made up of digital information that can be text, video, software, and so on, and often some mixture of all of these things.

Take for example the movie *Casablanca* from 1942. If you wanted to watch this movie, you could see if there are any websites that make it available. You might check a pay website if you have a subscription, like Netflix .com, and see if it is available to watch online. Or you check free video sites such as YouTube.com or Vimeo.com to see if it is there. Note that if it is on one of these sites, it has probably been uploaded illegally, or just in parts. On YouTube, for example, you can find many clips from *Casablanca* but not the entire film (likely because of copyright/legality issues). But what else? You can use wikipedia.org to read about the making of the film and research the historical context of the story. You can use imdb.com to see the full cast and crew, in addition to many other details about the film, including run time, filming locations, trivia, and so on, as well as to see pictures. You can run a Google image search to look at more still photos from this film, or at other pictures of Humphrey Bogart and Ingrid Bergman. Via imdb.com or other sites with discussion capability, you could join a message or discussion board to talk about this film. Using other websites, you can search for reviews of the film, read articles about the film by academics, or get suggestions for what else to watch. Go back to YouTube to watch Ingrid Bergman's acceptance speech for one of her three Academy Awards, and try not to get sucked in watching other actors accepting awards.

Zooming out even more, you might look at high-resolution maps of the city of Casablanca. You can look at satellite photos of the city. You would see what the airfields of Casablanca look like from the air and compare to the famous farewell scene.

Using Yelp.com, you could see if a real Rick's Cafe American exists there. Using an airline's website or Kayak.com, you could price out a plane ticket to Casablanca and even buy one. Then you can find out what the weather is in Morocco this month, and use yet other websites to find a list of things to pack. End your frenzy of digital information by checking out what kind of visa you would need to enter the country.

But before we get too far down an Internet rabbit hole of ever-spiraling searches, let's pause for a moment. These are all examples of what people use the Internet for, and we still have barely scratched the surface. If you can think of something to do, to watch, to read, to look up, or to experience, you can probably do it online.

Let's now look in more specific detail at just three of the most common ways people use the Internet.

1. **General Personal Communication.** Email should top this list, along with personal, social networking. People use the Internet to write and receive letters from other friends, family, or businesses in the form of email. People log onto Facebook, Twitter, or other social media sites to share photographs and information with their families, and to tell the whole world that they are fighting with their boyfriend or what they had for dinner. People might keep an online journal or blog showing their favorite outfits, past vacation spots, or workout techniques. Think of using the Internet the same way you would use a telephone: to get access to other people as well as to institutions and organizations whom you need. Whether sending a thank you note to your parents for taking you to lunch or trying to send a long-lost classmate your first note in 35 years, these are some of the personal things you can do online.

2. **Online Dating.** According to recent estimates, huge percentages of couples meet online. There are traditional dating sites where one fills out a profile and then receives matches based on desired criteria. Some of these sites charge money for the matching service, and some are free. Other sites do not make matches, but simply allow you to search through profiles with very specific criteria: all the single Indian heterosexual women who like dogs, for example, or white men within a specific mile radius of your zip code who

like to cook. These sites allow folks to send each other messages through the site, so you can avoid giving out any truly private information such as your email address or phone number. Participants can trade photographs or other information with relative privacy. In addition to these dating sites, there are many sites that function more like simple classified ads where the emphasis is less on romance and more on in-person meeting. Additionally, there are smartphone apps that can show you, using the phone's GPS, how many feet or miles away from a potential romantic partner you are.

3. **Banking.** Most banks have websites from which you can check your bank balance, input and pay bills, or transfer money between your accounts. Using banking websites or apps, you can access images of checks written or deposited, keep track of your purchases, and receive real-time balances. A nice feature of most banks is that the secure web portals also have many links to customer-service information, either by chatting with a live representative of the bank or writing emails for help. Often credit card companies feature a place to apply for a lower interest rate or chose a new due date. Managing your money online can give you more powerful tools and greater access to your accounts.

DIGITAL LITERACY

Mozilla's web literacy standards (from October 2013) are a convenient place to start talking about digital literacy. Mozilla is a software company that makes the popular and powerful Firefox browser. The community of software developers and Internet users engaged with improving how the Internet—especially Internet browsing—works and how users interact with it has drafted a set of web literacy standards. While these web literacy standards are constantly subject to further refinement and improvement and should be considered living documents, they are organized under three broad headings: exploring, building, and connecting. This book focuses on the first and the third: exploring and connecting. These are the two standards of web literacy that beginning computer users most need to develop. More advanced users will find the literacy standards grouped under building more familiar. While the most ideal teaching Internet basics situation would leave you with students and participants engaged with "building" literacies such as composing for the web, remixing, or design and accessibility, among others, the truth is that engaging with these literacies presumes certain levels of general and digital literacy that most beginning users will not have.

This book shows you ways of incorporating many of these standards into your computer basics instruction. In particular, the workshops detailed and explained here cover the navigation standard (which includes web mechanics, search, credibility, and security) and the connecting standard (which includes sharing and collaborating, community participation, privacy, and open practices). Read more about these groupings and individual standards at https://webmaker.org/standard.

Navigation standard, web mechanics = Chapter 1, Chapter 5

Navigation standard, search = Chapter 5

Navigation standard, credibility = Chapter 5

Navigation standard, security = Chapter 1, Chapter 3, Chapter 6, Chapter 7

Connecting standard, sharing, and collaborating = Chapter 4, Chapter 7

Connecting standard, community participation = Chapter 7

Connecting standard, privacy = Chapter 1, Chapter 3, Chapter 6, Chapter 7

SPECIAL NOTE ON DEVICES

This manual works best for teaching users on desktop or laptop computers managed by the librarian or other library staff. Using library computers helps the librarian stay in the electronic environment in which she or he is most comfortable or experienced, and may afford instructors the opportunity to preload web pages or bookmark links for the hands-on activities. But many library users also already have their own smartphones, tablets, netbooks, or laptops they are already using to some degree of proficiency, and may insist on bringing their own devices. Within limits, instructors should encourage this!

When a user can learn on her own laptop or tablet, the learning objectives may stick more quickly because she is learning in her most comfortable environment, and the goals might be more easily reproduced later without instructor help. Additionally, it might increase your capacity for instruction by making more devices available to more library users. To that end, while this book is designed for users using library computers, watch for special adaptations and common problems that may arise on personal devices. These will be found under the heading "Common Pitfalls" in each individual chapter. In general, though, watch for the following issues:

- Power supply and workspace: If users are bringing in their own devices, they will need clear workspaces adjacent to where you are conducting training. If you already have a small computer lab with no extra desks, this might not be possible. Users will also need access to power outlets.
- BYOD: If BYOD (bring your own device) is big in your library and might even outnumber patrons using library computers, encourage it by scheduling a special BYOD training time where all the participants are on their own devices.
- Wi-Fi access: Sometimes accessing a library's Wi-Fi connection on personal laptops or tablets necessitates logging in with a library card number or being close to the router. Plan ahead and give yourself some extra time to make sure patrons can use the library Wi-Fi on their personal device and that the Internet signal is robust enough to work with the sites you will need in the training.
- Operating systems and software differences: If your library computers are top of the line iMacs and users bring in 10-year-old Windows laptops, there

are going to be vocabulary differences and slight operational differences (like using double click versus single click, or using the "right click" option). Be aware of these differences, but throw some caution to the wind: one of the primary goals of this manual is to prepare library professionals to help library users access and use digital information effectively. As long as the device in question has an Internet browser (and they all do) and can connect to the Internet, these plans will work! This guide is intended primarily for librarians and learnings using PCs running Windows, and can easily be used in a variety of versions (from Windows XP up through Windows 8.1). If your technology instruction lab devices (or library computers) are Macs, you will need to make some common-sense adjustments to these plans, especially in terms of what particular buttons look like and where they are located. Adapt as needed.

HOW TO USE THIS BOOK

Each chapter describes a workshop teaching basic computer skills, and will start with a general description of the content covered, how to best deliver the content (for example, in how many sittings), and how long the workshop should be. You should feel free to adapt these workshops how they will work best in your library environment. Most can be effectively delivered in one- to two-hour blocks on individual days, or over a series of days for a deeper instructional experience.

1. *After-Class Competencies*

    This section lists the competencies and Internet skills users will have practiced and (perhaps) mastered in the workshop. Use these in the form of pre- and post-questionnaires as one way of evaluating your instructional workshops.

2. *Before Class*

    These workshops are designed as presentation-style workshops where you, the instructor, has a computer whose display is projected on a screen. If your setup does not have an instructor PC, make handouts. Consider making handouts anyway. Many beginning computer users try and write down every word you say. That will never work. A handout helps them feel secure when you let them know that they should just experience the workshop and not worry about getting things right the first time. In my experience, the same beginner can do a computer basics (Chapters 1–3) series over and over again, gaining more and more expertise being guided through the same material.

    This section lists the things you should do to prepare to teach these work-shops. These tasks could vary from selecting books from the collection to promote and display to registering sample and dummy email addresses. Be sure to give yourself at least a day in advance, and take a practice run through your slides and series of clicks, if you are projecting an instructor PC or device.

    You'll also find a number of *key concepts* in this section, which are defined and contextualized in depth and are meant to be both preparatory material for an instructor, as well as a reference during class. Instructors should familiarize themselves with these key concepts and be prepared to share them with participants.

3. *Common Problems and How to Solve Them*

In this section, I have drawn on my experiences teaching these workshops and atempted to identify pitfalls I experienced and problem solved. See these as inevitable in some cases—there is no frustration like a patron being irrevocably locked out of a Gmail account after an hour of trying—but also as contingencies to plan against.

Beginning computer users need to practice for hours and hours, far more than they actually have access to your library computers. It happens often that someone who has never used a computer will show up when other people are ready to type their resumes. Attempt to accommodate them by relying on handouts and self-guided courseware (see Appendix A).

4. *Workshop Plan*

This workshop plan presents and explains the key concepts in a logical and progressive way. While you are welcome to (and I would encourage you to!) vary the text to suit your personality and community, you can also stick closely to this plan as a script and present a clear and informative workshop. *Show users* means, if possible, to show them on live computer. If not, use the *slides* as handouts. Most of this section is presentation-heavy. As the chapters progress, so do the Internet and computer skills your workshop participants have practiced. To that end, the workshops themselves become more hands-on once users have experienced the Computer Basics series (Chapters 1, 2, and 3).

5. *Hands-On Activities*

These additional learning activities will reinforce the skills learned in the workshop. Use these exercises with participants to practice the skills you just taught and to apply their understanding and work through problems. Use these as time permits and as extension activities. Because Chapters 1, 2, and 3 are less participatory in the training script, their hands-on activities are essential.

1

Browsers and Getting Online

This class will work best in a two-hour time slot, repeated frequently. First-time users need as much repetition as possible, and you will find that the same users will want to take this class again and again. For that reason, anything longer than two hours is too long. If necessary, you could also teach this in two one-hour blocks, although the amount of start-up time for a beginner means that you should repeat the first 15 minutes every new hour.

AFTER-CLASS COMPETENCIES

After class, participants should be able to:

- Open a browser window and use tabbed browsing
- Type in a web address
- Travel to a new uniform resource locator (URL), and back
- Distinguish an email address from a web address

BEFORE CLASS

- Prepare the PCs by turning them on, but do not open any browsers.
- If possible, have several different browsers available with their icons in the start menu (on a PC) or as shortcuts on the desktop. Use at least Mozilla Firefox, Google Chrome and Microsoft's Internet Explorer (PC), and Safari (Mac), and consider trying others such as Opera.
- Prepare bookmarks for your library's website. (*Note:* You can load other bookmarked links, but part of this lesson is navigating web addresses and making bookmarks, so don't do all of the work for them!)

- Test projector and make sure the instructor desktop is visible *or* prepare a deck of slides or handouts.
- Consider making available a Sample Mouse 101 Handout (see Appendix C).

This lesson covers computer and Internet basics. It is meant for library users who have never used the Internet before, or who have only used the Internet a few times. This probably also means that they have not used a computer or Internet device before, and many of your first-time learners will not be mouse and computer proficient. If you are interested in starting your Internet and computer basics curriculum with a lesson on using the mouse and keyboard, refer to Appendix C.

Beginning Internet users often have a hard time mediating between the abstract world of digital information and all of its terms (click, drag, tap, copy/paste, open a window) and what those terms mean in the physical/analogue world. In addition to understanding that double-clicking an icon means opening a program (What's an icon? what's a program? Aren't we in a library program right now? Is that like an app?), but that single-clicking just selects a button or places the cursor, users may also be struggling with how to use only the mouse and keyboard to perform these actions. Be patient, and whenever possible, use the actual terms (click on that icon) rather than colloquialisms (tap on that thing there). Do not be afraid to describe things on the screen (an icon that looks like a beach ball, for Chrome; click on that red shape that looks like a stop sign), but whenever possible, use and repeat the specialized vocabulary in question.

KEY CONCEPTS

The following *key concepts* will be presented to learners below in the training script, slides, and hands-on activities. Familiarize yourself with them, and refer to them as needed.

Browsers

Browsers are software programs that translate computer code into words, pictures, music, and video. Browsers are the primary way that we humans, and especially we humans in this class, will interact with web pages.

Web Pages

Web pages are how people interact with the Internet. Websites are made up of individual web pages organized together and linked together. Every time you go online, you start at one web page. Navigating the Internet means that you are traveling (electronically) from one web page to another. That's why you will notice that you use Back and Forward buttons on your Internet browser to bring you back along the pages you have already visited.

Web Addresses

Stick with this traveling metaphor, and imagine how it is that your computer can find one specific web page out of the millions of pages out there. Internet users navigate by knowing specific web addresses or knowing how to search for them.

Domain Names

The .com shows us that it is a commercial website. This suffix is an example of what is called a domain; other domains can show that a site is an educational site (.edu), a nonprofit organization (.org) or that it is a site from a country outside the United States (.co.uk for the United Kingdom or .jp for Japan). In the early days of the Internet, these different domain kinds were reliable. But nowadays, they might just indicate a different marketing strategy. That is to say, you should not always assume that .org means a nonprofit or that .edu is a school or college.

In addition, some popular domains, such as .tv (for the country Tuvalu) have been sold to U.S. television companies because it makes good marketing for a TV show's web address to end with .tv. Similarly, there was a failed attempt to make all pornographic websites register with the domain .xxx to make them easier for filtering software to block.

The name in the middle, in this case "amazon," is the name of the website.

Email Addresses

In addition to web address (think house numbers), Internet users must also cope with email addresses. Email will be covered in depth in Chapter 4, but be sure that users leave your introductory class understanding that web addresses and email addresses exist, and be able to distinguish between their forms.

Email addresses are much more like phone numbers in that they are a way to reach a specific person or individual. So if web addresses are house numbers, email addresses are phone numbers. Remember that you would never type a house number into your phone and expect the call to go through. Similarly, typing an email address into a web browser won't make anything happen.

Distinguishing between email addresses and web addresses is as easy as the @ symbol. If an address has an @, it's an email address. If not, it's probably a web address.

Tabs and Tabbed Browsing

Browser windows can only show one website or web page at a time. You can open up multiple browser windows to use more than one website at once, but that makes the computer desktop crowded and confusing very quickly.

Links

Links are the way we describe ways to get from one web page to another. When people make web pages, they create links that go from one page to the next. Remember, the Internet is made up of web pages. Links are ways to travel from one to the next. You can usually recognize in a couple of ways:

→ They are usually underlined, and often are blue.

→ When you hover over them with the mouse, the mouse pointer will change shape, and you may even be able to see the address to which it links in the lower left-hand corner of the browser.

Links are ways to manage traffic to and from a web page. They are also ways to send traffic from one place to another. So it is not hard to imagine that sometimes web page designers (think shopping scams and pornographic websites) will sometimes disguise a link so you cannot really recognize what you are clicking on, and before you know, it you are on an entirely different website. Remember you can always hit the Back button!

COMMON PROBLEMS AND HOW TO SOLVE THEM

- Mouse/keyboarding trouble: some users will not be able to master using the mouse and keyboard. Try and divert them to a Mousercize website they can work through independently until their mousing skills let them keep up. See also Appendix A for other suggested practice sites.

WORKSHOP PLAN

Welcome and Introductions

Introduce yourself, and ask participants to do the same, also commenting on what kind of things they hope to learn.

Ask them if they have ever used a computer before, and if your group is small, allow users to share. Then ask them if they have ever used the Internet before.

Note how many people do not raise their hands. This will give you an idea of the general level you need to address; and it is also your time to triage the situation, if needed.

If hands don't go up, you might say something like this:

"I bet many of you have, and you might not have even known. Have you called your credit company or bank and used their automated system? Have you checked out a book from the library using a self-checkout machine? Or used at ATM machine recently? You were probably using the Internet without even knowing it. Because all the Internet really is information that lives on and is accessed through computers."

1. Browsers

Browsers are computer programs, or apps, that let us look at the Internet. These programs show us web pages. They appear like windows on the desktop of the computer. Think of them as windows: you have to open them, you can make them bigger or smaller depending on how much of the page you want to see, and when you are done looking, you have to close them.

Double-click on the browser icon to open a browser window. (Indicate the name of the browser, Firefox, Chrome, Safari, etc.)

Browsers = computer programs that let us look at/read/interact with the internet

Figure 1.1 Browsers are computer programs that let us access the Internet.

Pointer = ↖

Cursor = | (blinking)

Hand =

Figure 1.2 The mouse will variously appear as a pointer, a cursor, or a hand to navigate a computer window.

Show Users: The Pointer, the Cursor, and the Hand

You will interact with the computer using the mouse. As you move it around, that pointer will move around on the screen. Try it! That pointer can have three different shapes when you are using the Internet, and all three are important.

> The **pointer** lets you click on things and drag them. (Don't worry about these "things" yet: we will get there!)
>
> When you hover (hold the mouse pointer over) something that is a link, the pointer turns into a **hand**.
>
> When there is a place online where you need to type something, such as an address bar or to fill out a form, it becomes a **cursor**.

Ask participants to bring their mouse pointers overtop the address bar at the top of the window. Point out that as they do this, it turns into a vertical cursor bar. Now as them to click, and notice that this transfers the cursor into the text box. Ask if they see the blinking vertical in the URL bar, and instruct them that they can now type.

2. Web Pages

The next step is to visit a web page. With the cursor still blinking, ask class members to type and notice the letters appear in the address bar. Visit the popular search engine, google.com by typing: G—o—o—g—l—e—period-c—o—m. Now press go or the green arrow at the far right of the address bar or hit the Enter button on the keyboard.

The class will see that they have just traveled from one page to another. Once they are on the website google.com, explain that the Internet works because there are billions or web pages that are all hooked together, sending and receiving information to each other.

Computer users can navigate by typing in a specific Internet address *exactly as it appears* or by searching for a web page. In addition, they can follow your own path online using a browser's Back and Forward buttons.

Back will bring them back to the website they were just on. Have the class try this. Point out how they traveled back.

Forward brings them ahead. Ask them to try it—they should be back on Google.

Refresh is also a useful browser button. If a web page "stalls out," won't load, or loads with an error message, this button may help. It asks the Internet for the web page all over again, and this time it might work.

3. Domain Names and Web Addresses

Web pages have web addresses called URL (which stands for uniform resource locator). They are precise and exact locations on millions and millions of computers all over the world, which is why they have to be exact.

Address Bars and Browser Navigation

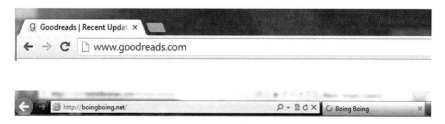

Figure 1.3   Two examples of a URL, or address, bar.

Tell users to imagine that the block they live on or the town or neighborhood they live in represents the Internet. Every single one of the houses on the block should represent a website. So, if you want to visit the Murphy family down the street, you know you have to go down and knock on #14, their house number. Punching #14 into your phone does not do it. And knocking on #11 or #19 will get you a different set of neighbors. So, if you want to visit google.com, you need to type that address exactly.

Computers are actually "dumb." They cannot and do not think for us, so they are only ever as useful as we make them. If you tell a computer to turn left where there is no left turn available, it just won't work. It doesn't know how to say, "oh, that road is closed or that bridge was swept away, find an alternate route." It will just sit there and wait for you to tell it what to do.

Next, explain that many of us are familiar with the basic form of an Internet address:

www.amazon.com

The www tells the computer where to look (on the World Wide Web). For the most part, the www., along with the http:// (which stands for hypertext transfer protocol), which also tells a computer where to look for the address, can be eliminated. Occasionally, some websites are registered differently, so when in doubt, use the www.

The different endings—those two and three letters that come after the "name" of the web page are called domains. Almost anyone can buy and register any kind of domain, but mostly.edu are for educational organizations, schools, and colleges, and .org are for organizations. .Com stands for commercial, as in business, and you will also see ones such as .tv, .biz, and so on. Websites from different countries also have different domains, for example, co.uk for United Kingdom, .de for Germany, or .za for South Africa. Whenever possible, notice the address and domain of the page you are surfing. It can give you more information.

Returning to the metaphor of the block or street, ask the participants to imagine they live on Sycamore Street, which has the domain .syc. So the Murphy family might have their web page at murphy.syc or 14.syc; however, the Browns, who run both their family website out of their house at #19 Sycamore, as well as a dry cleaning business might have two different address: their personal one at brown.syc but one for the dry cleaning business at brown.com or brown.biz. In addition, Grandfather Brown might run his own website at 19.syc. Bear with this convoluted example to understand that:

1. Organizations or individuals might have any many websites as they wish. They might look exactly the same but have different addresses, or they might be completely different websites with different or similar addresses.

2. Scammers or squatters might put up a fake website to catch web traffic from inexperienced users. Let's say you want to visit amazon.com. You might accidentally type amazpn.com.

If I were an entrepreneur with a pretty low level of ambition, I might put up a fake site at amazpn.com that sells advertisements that make money every time and unsuspecting user accidentally types in the wrong

Forms of Web Addresses

www.19.syc

www. 14.syc

www.brown.syx

www.brown.biz

Figure 1.4   Sample Internet addresses.

Spelling Counts!

www.amazon.com vs

www.amazpn.com

Figure 1.5   Spelling counts!

name. This might sound far-fetched, but with billions of people all over the world visiting millions or billions of websites every hour, someone can actually make a buck (or many thousands of bucks) this way.

Mention that safety from Internet scams will be covered in a later lesson.

Next, ask class to return to their web browsers and the pages they have open in it, Google.com. Google is an example of a search engine, a special website that searches for other websites.

For example, some addresses are unknown or impossible to remember. This lets you use words that describe what you are looking for to find sites

Search Engines = special websites that help you search for other websites

Google.com
Yahoo.com
Bing.com
Dogpile.com

Figure 1.6   Search engines are special websites that help you search for other websites.

that you did not even know existed. If you want to find the website for
NASA's Jet Propulsion Lab's website for really cool photographs from the
Mars rovers, you could know that the address is:

http://mars.jpl.nasa.gov/msl/multimedia/images/

Or, because that's a pretty intricate web address with lots of parts that are
hard to remember, you should instead use a search engine to find it.

Have participants navigate to google.com, and then type in "nasa jet
propulsion lab mars rover." Google uses the words you put in to search
billions of web pages and then returns to you, in a list, all the pages it
thinks match.

4. Email Addresses vs. Web Addresses

The next topic is brief but important: the differences between web addresses and email addresses.

Explain that users may be tempted to try and check their email by typing
their email address into the URL/address bar on a web browser. This won't
work! It is like typing in 14 Sycamore Street into your phone instead of 215
555 3320, or whatever. Email addresses are used to reach individual email
accounts. Web addresses are the home addresses of web pages.

Note: There is much more on email in a later lesson but this is already a
key distinction users should learn.

5. Links

Remind the class how they had the pointer, the cursor, and the hand
above? Now direct their attention to the hand. Remind them that the Internet is made up of billions of web pages "hooked" together. Online, those

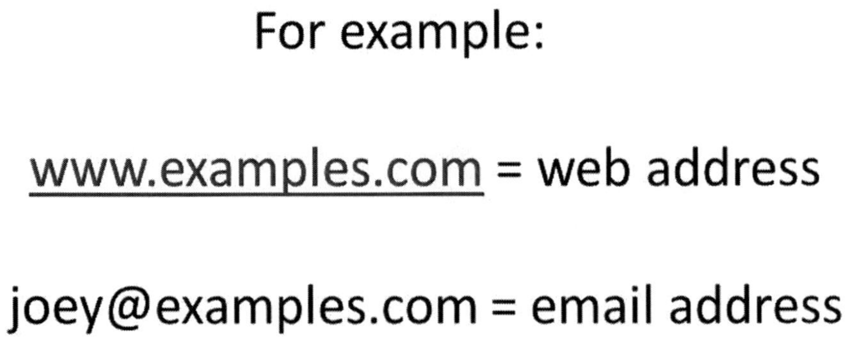

For example:

www.examples.com = web address

joey@examples.com = email address

Figure 1.7 Telling web addresses from email address is a key skill for beginning
Internet users.

Links = blue and underlined

List of elected and appointed **female heads of state** - Wikipedia, the ...
en.wikipedia.org/.../List_of_elected_and_appointed_**female_heads_of_st**... ▾
This is a list of women who have been elected or appointed **head of state** of their
respective countries since the mid 20th century. The list does not include ...
List of female heads of state - List of female representatives ... - Notes - See also

List of elected or appointed **female heads** of government - Wikipedia ...
en.wikipedia.org/.../List_of_elected_or_appointed_**female_heads**_of_go... ▾
For female leaders of presidential systems, where there is no separate head of
government, please see the List of elected and appointed **female heads of state** ...

Female world leaders currently in power - Filibuster Cartoons
www.filibustercartoons.com/charts_rest_**female**-leaders.php ▾
A comprehensive list of all **female** leaders in office around the world, including ... a
female governor general representing Queen Elizabeth as **Head of State**.

Current **Female** Leaders - Worldwide Guide to Women in Leadership
www.guide2womenleaders.com/Current-Women-Leaders.htm ▾
Oct 20, 2013 - Also see Chronological List of **Female** Presidents, ... Queen Elizabeth
used to be **Head of State** in most of the countries in the Commonwealth.

Figure 1.8   These are the first seven results in a Google search.

connections are called links. Links are parts of a web page that, when you click on them, bring you to a different web page. They can be images or text. If they are text, they usually look blue or underlined.

Now have everyone try it! First, tell them to hover over the Google search bar. They should then click so they can put the blinking cursor in the box and type "Library advocacy." Hit enter. This page of results is full of links. Look at them and try some out. Point out: how the pointer turns into a hand over a link. Direct users to click on a link and notice that the browser is now showing that new web page. They can click Back to go back to the page of Google results.

6. Tabs

Tabs are a way to have multiple web pages open at once.

For example, if you are paying bills online, you might want your bank website open at the same time you are on the electric company or credit card company website. Or you might want to have a song or video playing in one window—or tab—while you check your email in another. Many users prefer to open up new tabs in the same window to cut down on the visual clutter.

Demonstrate how to click open a new tab. This is a great time to demonstrate the right-click button.

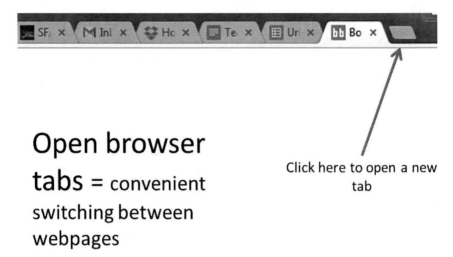

Figure 1.9   An example of multiple tabs open in the same browser window. Click each tab to see the web page.

Tell users to hover over a link, right-click, select "Open in a new tab," and click the left-hand mouse button.

They should then click on the little square button to open a new tab, and notice they now have two URL address bars to work with. Show class how to click back and forth between the old tab and the new one.

HANDS-ON ACTIVITIES

A. Open the web browser of your choice and point out the following features:

- Address bar (and Go button if using Internet Explorer)
- Back and Forward buttons
- Minimize, Maximize, and Close buttons (upper right-hand corner if on a PC, upper left on a Mac)

Instruct users to type your library's web address into the bar and hit enter or click go. Did they travel to your library website?

If yes, move on.

If no, direct them to double check for spelling errors or spaces between the words.

B. Identify a link from your library's homepage to another page on your website. Direct users to click the link. Ask them to notice:

- The web address/URL: if they stayed on your site, they probably went from something like samplelibrary.org to samplelibrary.org/calendar or samplelibrary.org/catalog.

C. Identify a link that takes users from your library's homepage/domain to another page. This could be any local resources link, or something from your library's blog or offsite Tumblr.

Point out:

- The animation that goes along with a browser "working." This could be a wavy effect over Internet Explorer's "E," a status bar filling up across the bottom of the browser window, the circle animation in the upper left-hand corner of the Chrome browser, among others. Tell your class that this indicates that their computer is exchanging information with other computers over the Internet. When they see that is working, they don't need to click again because they are on their way. But if it gets stuck and this animation or status bar hangs in the same spot for more than one to two minutes, there is probably something wrong. In that case, they should hit refresh.

D. Show a screenshot of the browser's navigation menu. Be sure to highlight and then demonstrate how to

- Go forward
- Go back
- Refresh

In a live browser window, demonstrate. This is a great time to remind folks about the following:

- Minimize button
- Maximize button
- Close button

And to show them that part of the screen magnified or via screenshot.

E. Ask participants, Are these email addresses or web addresses?

mayor@city.gov
propertytaxbills.cityhall.gov
articles.news.com
reporterannie@news.com
www.whitehouse.gov
president@whitehouse.gov
nytimes.com
bbc.co.uk
feedback@bbc.co.uk
rehka.andrews@musterman.org

F. For each of these email addresses below, ask class to determine what kind of organization employs these people or where are they located, using the domain names to find out. Remind class, the domain name is what comes after the @ sign.

gstein@harvard.edu
alice.b.toklas@steinfoundation.org

barnesj@nightwood.com

nathaliebarney@leftbankbooks.com

BarneyN@leftbankpublishing.org

austen.jane@wemberly.biz

hcandersen@littlemermaid.com

hans.c.andersen@littlemermaid.dk

writers@nyc.rr.com

helpdesk@technologylibrary.co.uk

Instruct users to find the domains for each of the email addresses above by replacing the name@ with www., so in the first example, users would navigate to www.harvard.edu.

Tell users that they have just done some of their first Internet sleuthing!

G. This is also a great time to reinforce tabbed browsing. Ask users to

- Navigate to the library homepage, and then to
- Open the library's online public catalogue in a new tab.

2

Email

This chapter is about the wild world of email: traditional server clients, webmail services like Gmail or Yahoo, as well as for-pay services. It should be taught in one sitting, and can be taught in an hour. In one sitting, users should at least be able to register an email account and send/receive their first emails.

AFTER-CLASS COMPETENCIES

After this class, users should be able to:

- Give their full email address
- Log in to their webmail with their complete email address and password
- Find and read new mail in their inbox
- Reply to an email
- Locate email in their sent, drafts, or deleted folder
- Detect spam or phishing scams

BEFORE CLASS

- Register an email address with the service of your choice to use as a sample, and to use during class. This address will not only give you a working email address to send and receive emails from the learners in the email workshop, but will also give you as the instructor an up-to-date look at the specific details for signing up with whatever service you select. Some services to consider are gmail.com, yahoo.com, outlook.com, mrmail.com, mail.com, or gmx.com.
- Print up blank wallet cards/business-card sized pieces of paper for learners to write their email address, their passwords, and the uniform resource locator (URL) they will use to access the service. Note that this runs somewhat counter to conventional wisdom about privacy, because the wallet card will

have both username and password on it. I found that, for beginning computer users without much access, this is the only way they will remember the username/password combination days or weeks later. An ideal learning environment is a typical computer lab, with one instructor computer connected to a projector or mirror display.

- Connect and test projector to ensure that the instructor desktop is visible.
- Print up email wallet cards to distribute. (See Appendix C.)

This lesson covers email. It is meant for library users who are new to or experienced with the Internet, and presumes that users do not already have an email address. You will find that, at this point, most users have had some experience with email, but try to assess their situation to discover who already has a working email address they can log in to. Be sure to split your group into two if there are many users who can already log in. Direct them to log in to their email accounts and to spend the first 30 minutes of class clicking around, exploring, sending you a practice email, or drafting a list of questions to ask. The users who are using this class to sign up for an email account will need at least 30 minutes, if not more, to register an account.

If needed, refer to Appendix A for information about teaching basic mousing or keyboarding, if that is more appropriate for some users at this stage.

KEY CONCEPTS

The following *key concepts* will be presented to learners in the training script, slides, and hands-on activities. Familiarize yourself with them and refer back to this list as needed.

What Is Email?

Email stands for electronic mail. It is designed to emulate "snail" or post-office mail in a digital environment, and enables users to send and receive private information online. To send and receive, users need an email account or an email address. While these terms are somewhat interchangeable, underline to learners that "email address" is the literal "username@domainname.com" address one would give out if she or he wants to be contacted via email. "Email account" refers to the whole apparatus: a website or URL that hosts your account, the username, and password one needs to log in to the website to access the email, as well as the features (sending, receiving, retrieving).

Usernames and Email Addresses

Distinguishing between usernames and entire email addresses can be frustrating and unclear to beginning users. Usernames are the personal part of an address: firstnamelastname, or in my case, joelnichols. Some organizations, schools, or companies tend to use the same pattern for generating usernames, which might include firstname.lastname (joel.nichols), lastnamefirstinitial (nicholsj), firstinitiallastname (jnichols), among others. But the username is just one part of the address. A complete email address uses a username plus the @ symbol plus a domain name: so, joel.nichols@teachinginternetbasics.com, for example. Remind users what we learned in the last lesson about email addresses, that they are easily compared to phone numbers because they are used to community between individuals (or several individuals) with relative privacy.

Inbox

An email inbox is where a user can find his or her email. New messages are always delivered to the inbox, and will stay in an inbox until users move them. Inbox interfaces are usually set up so users can see (1) who sent the message, (2) what the subject of an email is, and (3) a preview (the first few lines) of the email message itself. Usually, the email messages can be sorted in various ways in an inbox. These different ways of sorting can include by date, by subject, by who sent the message, and so on. Also, new and unread email messages are often marked as new and unread by appearing in bold type.

Composing Email/Writing a New Message

One of the primary functions of having an email account is being able to write and send emails. In various webmail services, users will find a button or link that says "Compose" or "New message" or "Write new email." When users click that button, a new blank message form will pop up. This form will have several blank fields for users to fill out. The most important of these are (1) the "to:" field, (2) the "subject:" field, and (3) the "message" field where the actual email goes.

The "To:" Field, "Cc:," and "Bcc:"

Emails work like paper letters in the sense that they are addressed to and sent to particular individuals. Much like making copies of a paper letter (think family holiday newsletter) and sending them in separate envelopes to all of your friends and family, emails can be sent to more than one recipient. Crucial for users is that the "to:" field needs to have at least one recipient. Users can also put more than one recipient's email address in this blank field. Webmail services vary, but usually, each additional email address needs to be separated from the one before it by a comma or semicolon. Double check which method your service uses. In addition, there are two other fields you can use for email addresses: "cc:," which stands for "carbon copy" and "bcc:" for "blind carbon copy." "Cc:" or "carbon copy" is the same as putting more than one email address in the "to:" field. When you enter an email address into the "bcc:" or "blind carbon copy" field, the person you are emailing will get a copy of the email, but they will not be able to see who else was copied on the email, that is, whom else you sent the email.

The Subject Field

It is important to use the subject field when sending an email. Because new emails in one's inbox show the sender and the subject line most prominently, it is crucial to give your emails a subject. Users can type anything into the subject field, but it is worth stressing that subject lines that accurately reflect the content of the email are probably more likely to be seen, opened, and read.

Sending Email

The main text of an email is called the body of an email. This is where the actual "letter" part of your electronic communication comes in. Once users have put an addressee in the "to:" field, written a subject in the "subject:" field, and composed the body of their email, they are ready to click "Send" for the email to go. This is often a button labeled "Send," but could be an icon or pictograph, depending on the webmail service you have chosen.

Attachments

Since the body of an email can really only hold text and textual information, other kinds of files can be sent along with an email as an attachment. A good physical-world analogue is enclosures in paper letter, when the sender alerts the person they are writing to that they have sent along additional documents, forms, or other information inside the same envelope. Almost any kind of file can be attached to an email and then sent to an intended recipient, although email services (both server client and webmail) usually have a size limit for attachments. The most common forms of an attachment are documents, picture, or photo files, or sometimes music or video. (The last two are less common because they usually require much larger file sizes, but users will find that people sometimes do send short videos or sound files as attachments.)

Note on very large attachments: If you want to send a file that is too big for your email service, there is an alternate method. Users can use a web tool such as Yousendit or Dropbox (yousendit.com or dropbox.com) to upload their file to a private and secure location on the Internet, and then use email to send the intended recipient a link to that file for download.

Sent Folder

Every email program and service automatically files a copy of any emails a user sends in a folder called "Sent mail." Much like the inbox, this folder is part of the major geography of any email service and is a good way for users to practice "finding" emails. This folder is useful because it maintains a record of sent email, including intended addressee(s), time and date, any files that might attached, and so on.

Trash or Deleted Items Folder

The third major "place" in an email account is the trash. This folder is where emails end up when a user deletes them from the inbox. The email is stored in the trash/deleted items folder. Depending on the email service in question, how long the deleted email remains available in this folder will vary. Some email services keep deleted items forever. Some prompt users to empty their trash folders when their email service runs out of space to store more emails, which deletes the message from a user's account forever.

Spam or Junk Mail

Much like junk letters arriving at your door promising to lower your monthly payments or sell you magazine subscriptions and grant you a million dollar sweepstakes, companies and individuals also use unsolicited email as a marketing and solicitation tool. These emails are often generated by computer programs and have no humans involved. These computer programs scour the Internet for individuals' email addresses and then send their junk mail indiscriminately. These are usually scams. Your email program probably has a "spam filter" that helps make sure these unwanted emails do not reach your inbox. (Perhaps cite some examples of spam filters here. And what if someone doesn't have a spam filter?)

Phishing

Phishing (pronounced like "fishing") is a specific kind of email spam where unscrupulous scammers try and trick user into clicking harmful links or entering information such as their banking, email, or social media passwords. When this "phishing" emails arrive in a user's inbox, they often appear to be legitimate communications from a bank or social media service like Facebook. They emulate the art and design of these sites, and encourage users to click a link and enter personal information.

COMMON PROBLEMS AND HOW TO SOLVE THEM

- Account authentication via second email address or phone number. Increasingly, webmail services are requiring that users enter a phone number that will (1) authenticate the account and (2) increase levels of security and require users to have a phone nearby when they want to log in to their email. In addition, some will ask for an additional email account. This is in case users forget or lose their passwords: the webmail service in question would send an email to the alternative email address provided that would help a user reset their password.

WORKSHOP PLAN

Welcome and introductions

Welcome participants and tell them they are going to learn about email, set up an email account, and start sending and receiving their first emails.

Ask participants to introduce themselves and say whether they already have an email account. If they do, determine whether or not they have a username and password. If they do not, you could run them through the password recovery procedure for their account. Or, in the interest of staying on time and helping all users at the same time, suggest that they register a new account.

Tell your class that email stands for "electronic mail." It is a way of sending messages to individuals and receiving private communications. Email messages can be comprised of text only—like a paper letter—or they can include images, just like getting a postcard in the regular mail. Tell participants to think of emails just like individual pieces of mail you would receive at home.

There is some additional vocabulary to learn, though. Email addresses are the specific computer code used to send something to a particular individual. Email accounts refer to the whole service, or the "place" on the Internet to log in to read mail, and also send and receive them. The goal of this class is to register participants with a webmail email account.

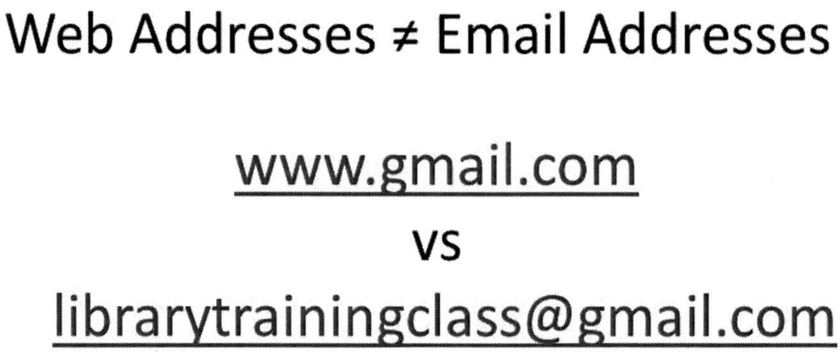

Web Addresses ≠ Email Addresses

www.gmail.com

VS

librarytrainingclass@gmail.com

Figure 2.1 Keep practicing until workshop participants are comfortable distinguishing between email address and web addresses.

Usernames and Email Addresses

Remind users to think remember the difference between web addresses (URLs) and email addresses, and that they were like the difference between someone's physical or mailing address and someone's telephone number. Well, much like a telephone number, which is made up of an area code, an exchange, and a four digit number, email addresses also have specific parts that help users recognize and use them. Email addresses are made up of three parts:

1. Usernames = this is an individual's unique "handle" or name
2. The @ (at) symbol = hold down the Shift key and press the "2" key to access @
3. The domain name = the webmail service or domain name of the email hosting service

Inform the class that in a few minutes they are going to pick email addresses, so they will be picking usernames. Ask them to begin thinking about what they want their email address to be. Keeping in mind that someone else might already have the username they would like, they should think of some alternatives. Some great options are some combination of your first and last names, with or without your middle initial, and usually with some numbers. Remember that these need to be easy enough for you to remember and for other people to remember as well.

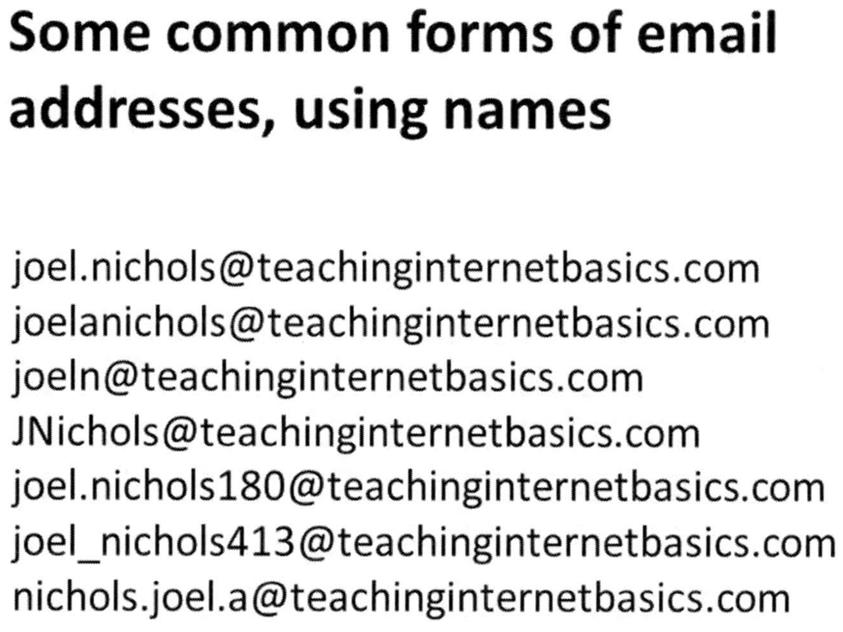

Some common forms of email addresses, using names

joel.nichols@teachinginternetbasics.com
joelanichols@teachinginternetbasics.com
joeln@teachinginternetbasics.com
JNichols@teachinginternetbasics.com
joel.nichols180@teachinginternetbasics.com
joel_nichols413@teachinginternetbasics.com
nichols.joel.a@teachinginternetbasics.com

Figure 2.2   Some common forms of email addresses based on a person's name.

On scrap paper, have participants write out some ideas for their email usernames. Remind them that the whole address will be something like username@emailservice.com, probably substituting in gmail.com or ymail .com, among others. They should start testing their desired names soon, though, because everything they want may already be taken.

On the live web browser, enter the URL of the email service you have chosen.

The following script walks you through both a gmail.com sign up as well as an outlook.com set up. Chose one of these, or another that works better for your learners.

Gmail.com

After accessing the website of the webmail service in question (here, Gmail), tell participants to click the "Create an account" button. The browser will now show a new page, which is made up of many blank fields. "Fields" or "blanks" are places in a web page where Internet users can type—or input—text.

Demonstrating this on the projected screen, instruct class to hover over the blank field until the mouse arrow becomes a vertical bar. Clicking in the field activates the blinking cursor. That is where they can type.

Starting with your first and last names, begin filling out every field. Here is a description of each field, with tips:

- Name (first and last): Whatever a user enters here will display when they send emails. Users do not have to use their "real" names, and should remember that they can register additional email addresses for different purposes. Advise them that if they want to use this email account for job applications or other business, they should use their actual and preferred names.

- Choose your username: This is the most integral part of your email address. Choose carefully! Notice that the last part of the address "@gmail.com" is already filled in.

- Create a password: You will use this password to log in to your email every day. It needs to be strong and you need to remember it. Consider writing it and your username on the card until you have memorized it. But keep it private. As you type in this field, you will see asterisks instead of the characters you are typing. This is to preserve your privacy.

- Confirm your password: Type the password again, exactly. This is a way computers double check that what you think you are typing for your password is what you are actually input.

- Birthday: Select the month from a drop down menu by clicking on the arrows at the right of the field. Then input the day and year with the number keys. *Note:* You are not obliged to use your real birthday.

- Gender: Although you cannot leave this empty, users can chose from male, female, or other.

- Mobile phone: Google services ask for a mobile phone number, but this field is optional. The phone number can be used to authenticate an email account on different computers. You can skip this step for now.

- Your current email address: Instead of a phone, users can also use a current email address to authenticate your new email account. You can also leave this field blank.

- Default homepage: This box will be automatically checked to let Google make itself the first page that appears when you open the browser. For those working on public library computers, this setting does not matter.

- Prove you're not a robot: This area has a box to check to skip this verification. The second part is called a "captcha." (See special note later.) For this captcha, click in the field labeled "Type the text" and type the numbers or letters in the pictures.

- Location: United States is preset but change it to whatever is appropriate. Click on the arrows at the right end of the field to access the alphabetical drop down menu.

- The final box on the form must be clicked. It acknowledges that the user has accepted the Google Terms of Service and Privacy Policy. Users should read these to know what they can expect from Google's use of their information.

Tell them that when they have filled out all the fields, they should click the blue button labeled "Next step."

If there are any problems with the form, the page will refresh with red lines around the fields with problems and a hint such as "you can't leave this empty," also in red.

Note on "robots": The "robots" in question here are not ones from the cutting edge of the military industrial complex or science fiction movies, but rather automated computer programs. The programs are coded to automatically register email addresses, which can later be used to send spam emails. Sometimes these are called spambots, as well.

Now you have an email address! Click through the welcome message on your screen, and you are in your inbox for the first time.

Note: This next section is email service-agnostic, which is to say that it will work for whatever webmail service (Gmail, Outlook, or others) that you have chosen to teach. While each service varies in what particular buttons are labeled, the basic functionality of all email accounts is the same.

On the overhead screen, show participants the inbox. Point out that if they look down the left-hand side of the screen, they can see the various folders that come built in to their mailboxes. These in outlook.com are Inbox, Archive, Junk, Drafts, Sent, and Deleted. In gmail.com, they are Inbox, Starred, Important, Chats, Sent Mail, Drafts, and Spam.

Advise the class that you will now walk through the main features of email, and then they can practice by sending each other email, reading it, and replying.

Explain that the inbox is where their new email arrives, and where it will stay until they move it somewhere. New messages usually show up in bold text, and users can see that the email service we just signed up with sent a welcome message.

Tell participants that they are going to compose a new email message and then send it. Once they have done that, they will check to make sure a copy of that message went into their "Sent" folders.

Have class click "New message" or "Compose email," which may be links or buttons. In most email services, this link or button will be located near the top of the window, probably toward the left-hand side.

In the "to:" field, ask participants to write the email address of the person they want to write to. For practice, they can use the library teaching account. Type this exactly: librarysampleemail@gmail.com. Remind them that in order to type the @ symbol, they will have to hold down the Shift key and strike the "2" key.

Next is the "subject:" field, where you give your email message a short introduction or write, in a couple words, the topic of your email. Remind the class that this is one of the first things that other people will see when their email reaches them, so strive to be informative. Have them type a subject.

Now ask participants to click into the biggest blank in the new email form, where the message itself gets typed. Remind them that emails are like letters, and although they do not need to follow a specific format, the more you stick to standard written format, the easier it will be for others to understand what they are emailing.

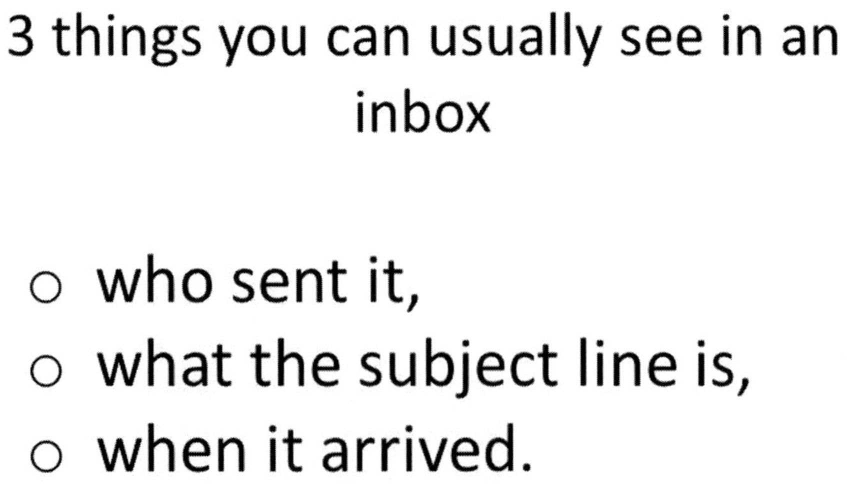

3 things you can usually see in an inbox

o **who sent it,**
o **what the subject line is,**
o **when it arrived.**

Figure 2.3   New emails in the inbox are usually displayed so users can see three things about it: (1) who sent it, (2) what the subject line is, and (3) when it arrived.

Blank Emails Look Like This:

TO:
SUBJECT:
[message field is blank]

Figure 2.4   A blank email, with spaces to fill out for "to:," "subject:," and the message itself.

Send a practice email to:

Libraryinstructor@gmx.com

Figure 2.5   Offer the sample email address in large, easy to read type.

Ask the class to write you an email! They can make up whatever, but to see the full effect of the email, they should write at least a salutation (such as "Dear Joel,") and a couple sentences.

When they're done, tell them to click send. This might be button labeled "Send" or a picture of email flying toward the right, or an arrow facing out of a box, or could be something else, too. Be sure you know what it looks like for your users.

If you are projecting your instructor desktop, show users how their email appeared in your inbox. Be sure to point out that the email is in bold type because it is new and unread, and show them how their name/email address appear on your email, and how much of the subject line you can see. Show them how to click on the mail to open it up and read it. Do all of this slowly, and be sure participants are looking away from their computer screens and at your sample teaching inbox.

Explain that you are going to reply to their emails, which means you are going to write an email back. Show the class their emails on your screen. Point to the options in the upper right corner in both Gmail and Outlook—and other services. These appear as an arrow pointing left, or the words "Reply to message" or something similar. Click "Reply."

Show users on the projected desktop that this opens up a new email message, but because you have clicked "Reply," note that the "to" field is already filled out. Remind users that this is an excellent feature because it makes it easy to get someone's email address exactly right. Instead of having to type in someone's address, the email program here is going to send an email back to the exact address this message came from.

Let the class know that you will now write a response to the email you received. Then type: "Dear Computer learner, thanks for attending our email basics class at the Library. We hope you visit again soon. Sincerely, Joel, your librarian and computer trainer." Mention that you will now click send.

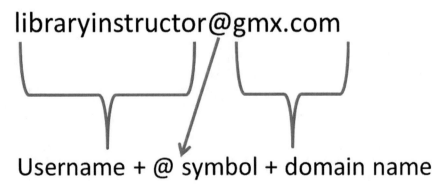

Anatomy of an email address

libraryinstructor@gmx.com

Username + @ symbol + domain name

Figure 2.6   The anatomy of an email address.

After you do, have participants click "Inbox" in their email accounts. Ask them if your reply arrived.

Encourage the class to keep practicing, following your same steps: click reply, and then write back. That will give everyone more practice sending our first emails.

On the projected screen, show class that their replies arrived.

Before starting more advanced email practice, walk the class through a few more features of their email address. Remind them that so far you have covered the inbox, reading a new email message, sending a new one, and replying.

On the projected screen, point out: sent, drafts, and trash/deleted.

Tell the participants that the next folder built into everyone's email to look at is the sent folder. A copy of every email you send is stored there, so you can double check that you actually sent something, when you sent it, and whether it had an attachment. Along the left-hand side of the account window, point out the option for "Sent." Have users click it and confirm that the two emails they sent are already in there. Ask if there are any other emails in there.

Next is "Drafts." This built-in folder is useful because it keeps an automatic copy of any email that you start writing but that you do not actually send. This preserves a draft copy of your message in case you want to (1) send it later, (2) your computer freezes or crashes before you can hit send, or (3) you are interrupted before you can finish. First, click "New mail" as we did earlier, and enter an email address. It can be a fake or incomplete one! Now, look for the option "Save as draft." Note that many services will automatically save any new emails as drafts, even if they have the "Save as draft" option additionally. Now, ask participants to click "Drafts" in list of links underneath the inbox link. Do they see the emails they just started? Tell them to click on it to reopen and finish composing, if they like.

Have the class return to their inboxes, click on the first email they received, which should have been the welcome email from the webmail service. When that email is open, have them click delete. That sends their email to a special trash, deleted items, or recycled folder. Instruct users that while it may still be recoverable from this folder, they should only delete things they can live without. To save it for later use, they should consider putting it in a different folder. Most of the class will agree that they can live without the welcome email, so have them click delete. They will see that it disappears from their inboxes and is now in their trash/deleted folders.

Instruct participants that they are now going to learn one last thing about sending email. When composing a new message, they will see that there are a variety of options for the "to:" field, where you write in the recipient's email address. In addition to "to:," you will see cc: and bcc:. In addition, there are two other fields you can use for email addresses: "cc:," which stands for "carbon copy" and "bcc:," for "blind carbon copy." "Cc:" or "carbon copy" is the same as putting more than one email address in the "to:" field.

When you enter an email address into the "bcc:" or "blind carbon copy" field, the person you are emailing will get a copy of the email, but they will not be able to see who else was copied on the email, that is, whom else you sent the email. Have the class practice by sending you another email, and put their own email address in the "bcc:" field. When they receive the blind carbon copy, they will notice that you cannot see that it was also sent to me.

Note: Some users may ask about sending and receiving attachments. This is covered at the end of Chapter 4 ("Typing and Documents"). Once users generate a document in that workshop, they can practice sending and receiving attachments. If you would like to include it as part of this lesson, you will need to prepare sample document or photo files for users to use, or will have to walk them through an exercise such as saving an Internet .jpeg (or other file) to the computer, and then relocating that file again to send as an attachment. Saving it for the end of the lesson on typing and documents locates these skills in a more organic place for learners, and lets them practice their skills without too much extra intervention or set up from the instructor.

HANDS-ON ACTIVITIES

A. Copy/paste email addresses

Direct users to any web page that contains a variety of email addresses. This could be any website with a contact us page listing email addresses. Some good sources to rely on might be your library's staff pages, or an academic department at a college or university. (House.gov and Senate.gov websites used to be a good source for this exercise, but, as is the trend with many websites to reduce spam, a listing of email addresses has been replaced with a contact form instead.) Once you have identified a list of addresses to choose from, show users how to select, copy, and paste an address. Encourage them to practice copying and pasting up to 10 addresses into new emails in their account.

B. More emails

Users should spend this class time emailing friends or associates, if they have those email addresses available. If they do not, consider helping them find a friend's email address via Facebook search, or simply asking them to email the library's sample instructional account instead.

C. Spam examples

Show the class a few examples of spam, or junk, emails (see samples that follow, or you may have some examples of your own to share.). Explain that some are just trash emails, where the senders are hoping you will click a link or respond; and some are active phishing scams meant to get you to give over credit card information, email addresses or passwords, and other personal information. Ask participants to examine them, and see if they can tell why these are scams or junk rather than genuine emails. Tell them to check the sender, the subject line, and the message text and figure out what seems fishy.

1. from: zainabbvandia@yahoo.com (via zmail.ru)
subject: dearest love

Dear lover,
   i believe you are the one i'm searching for Assalamu"alaikum, I am miss zainab from Iran, i am very happy to gone through your profile in this site, please reply to my email address (zainabbvandia@yahoo .com) so we can communicate easily to know each other the more, i promise to also send you my photo for you to know me.
   Remember that distance, religion or tribe does not matter in life but true affection is everything we need to live our life and be happy. Yours new found friend, Miss zainab (zainabbvandia@yahoo.com)

2. from: HQ-Canadian-Meds <noreply@sarahsclub.com>
   subject: Our mission is clear—to make as many people healthy, good looking and wealthy, as possible!
   message: Meds for Men, $1.39–5.92 | Meds for Women, $.52–8.45 | Antibiotics | Asthma and Allergy

3. from: capital one services (members@capitalonecreditcardonline)
   subject: reset account login
   message: Dear Capital One Customer,
   it has recently come to our attention that your account security could have been compromised! Please click the link below to reset your username and password.
   Sincerely, Capital One Security Team

4. from: Barrister James Samor <kenny_ivoire007@yahoo.com
   subject: VERY URGENTLY
   message: Dear,
   It is obvious that this proposal will come to you as a surprise; this is because we have not met before but I am inspired to sending you this email following the huge fund transfer opportunity that will be of mutual benefit to the two of us.
   However, I am Barrister James Samor, Attorney to the Late Engr. Ronald Campbell, a national of Northern American, who used to work with Shell Petroleum Development Company (SPDC) in Nigeria On the 11th of November, 2002. My client, his wife and their three children were involved in a car accident along Sagamu/Lagos Express Road. Unfortunately they all lost their lives in the event of the accident, since then I

have made several inquiries to several Embassies to locate any of my clients extended relatives, this has also proved unsuccessful. After these several unsuccessful attempts, I decided to trace his relatives over the Internet to locate any member of his family but of no avail, hence I contacted you, I contacted you to assist in repatriating the money and property left behind by my client, I can easily convince the bank with my legal practice that you are the only surviving relation of my client. Otherwise the Estate he left behind will be confiscated or declared unserviceable by the bank where this huge deposits were lodged. Particularly, the Bank where the deceased had an account valued at about $15 million U.S dollars (Fifteen million U.S. America dollars). Consequently, the bank issued me a notice to provide the next of kin or have the account confiscated within the next ten official working days. Since I have been unsuccessful in locating the relatives for over several years now. I seek your consent to present you as the next of kin to the deceased, so that the proceeds of this account valued at $15 million U.S dollars can be paid to your account and then you and me can share the money 60% to me and 40% to you. All I require is your honest cooperation to enable us see this deal through and also forward the following to me so that I can file an application of claim in your name to the transferring bank:

1. Your Full Name:
2. House Address:
3. Your Country:
4. Your Contact Telephone Number:
5. Your Age and Gender:
6. Your Occupation:

I guarantee that this will be executed under a legitimate arrangement that will protect you from any breach of the law.

Please get in touch with me VIA this my confidential email (barrjamessmor@hotmail.com)

Yours Faithfully,
Barrister James Samor.(SAN).

5. from: Robert Smith Special Offers (offer4you@mailcom.ru)
   subject: Claim your iPad now
   message: Your free iPad is waiting. Just click here to claim it.

D. Returned undeliverable

Sometimes a mail is returned almost as soon as a user has sent it, often because the address does not exist. This may be because a user has typed part of the address incorrectly, or part of the address is missing. Additionally, sometimes when a particular user's email account is no longer valid or is too full to accept new mail, users will receive an error message that reads "undeliver-able." Have users practice sending an email to an address they know is not valid (have them try this one: statusreport@howtoteachinternetbasics.org), and noticing what they receive in return. It will probably be an error message from their webmail service. The email will come from "Mail Delivery Subsystem" or "Microsoft Outlook" or the like, and will say something like "delivery failed due to bad address" or "failure notice; recipients not found."

3

Usernames and Logins

This chapter introduces the concepts of logging in, explains how web services require login accounts, demonstrates the kinds of sites that need passwords, and suggests ways for users to create usernames and passwords that are specific, private, and easy to remember. This chapter also covers some security and privacy topics, such as password recovery, creating a strong password, and identifying and securing against phishing scams. It should be conducted as a one-hour workshop.

AFTER-CLASS COMPETENCIES

After this class, users should be able to:

- Understand the key differences and uses of an email address as differentiated from an account name for another website
- Recognize and avoid weak passwords
- Generate a strong password
- Recognize and avoid phishing scams

BEFORE CLASS

- Register a library sample email address or your computer class email with the email service of your choice (such as Gmail).
- Print up blank wallet cards for learners to write username/password on, or use blank index cards.

KEY CONCEPTS

The following *key concepts* are presented to learners in the training script, slides, and hands-on activities. Familiarize yourself with them and refer back to this list as needed.

Usernames vs. Email Addresses

The idea of a username can confuse beginning users, because they already have an email username; and when they sign up for any other website or service that requires a username, they will also be asked to give their email addresses. Let users know that some web services allow an entire email address to be used for a username, but that some (e.g., banking services, social media sharing sites) may require something that is just a username or handle. Sometimes these are called "account" names.

Username Rules

Websites almost impose some rules on what a username consists of. There will likely be a limit on the number of characters allowed: often at least 6 or 8, and usually not more than 16–20 in total. In addition, they may require or disallow special characters such a punctuation or underscores. Usernames have to be unique, that is, you cannot pick something that someone else has already served. For this reason, it is a good idea for beginning users to come up with some of their own rules. The more consistent users are in picking the same or similar usernames for the sites they are using and logging into frequently, the easier it will be for them to remember their login details.

Strong Passwords

The quaint "old days" when email and other computer login passwords could be "password" or your first name are over. Increasing threats to security in the form of automated phishing and hacking robots mean that human users are up against computerized password hackers who are able to simply run through hundreds of thousands of combinations of letters and numbers until they get it right. Strong passwords are a user's best defense against computerized hacking. Strong passwords are hard-to-guess, appear to be a random collection of numbers, letters, and even punctuation, and also make use of uppercase and lowercase letters. Something like "bX57ut0p1A" is a lot harder to guess than "rover6284," for example.

Security Questions

Most Internet accounts—which should be taken very broadly to mean any website or app where you have to log in—are secured with a username and password. If users have forgotten their username or password or both, most accounts can be reset via email. Some accounts are also secured with security questions. These are secret questions the user selects and writes answers to. Then, when the user is seeking to change or recover a forgotten

Most Common (and Worst!) Passwords

#	Password
1	password
2	123456
3	12345678
4	abc123
5	qwerty
6	monkey
7	letmein
8	dragon
9	111111
10	baseball
11	iloveyou
12	trustno1
13	1234567
14	sunshine
15	master
16	123123
17	welcome
18	shadow
19	ashley
20	football
21	jesus
22	michael
23	ninja
24	mustang
25	password1

Source: http://splashdata.com/press/pr121023.htm

password, they must provide the answers anew. Of course, you can invent information or give false information for these questions, but if you cannot remember it several weeks, months, or years down the road, you will not be able to reset your password. If users are going to invent information here, remind them that they have to remember their (false) answers!

Examples of Common Security Questions

What is your favorite pet's name?

What street did you live on as a child?

What is your mother's father's first name?

What is the name of your first teacher?

What is your library card number?

What is the capital of the state where you were born?

What is your favorite color?

What is your least favorite ice cream flavor?

What were the last four digits of your first phone number?

What is your first child's nickname?

On what day of the week was your first child born?

What was your grandfather's profession?

What was your dream profession as a child?

What is the mascot of your favorite sports team?

What was the mascot of your high school basketball team?

What school did you attend for seventh grade?

What is your older sibling's middle name?

What was the name of your imaginary friend from childhood?

Who is your favorite author?

What was your first favorite book?

What is the name of the person whom you first kissed?

Where did you take your honeymoon?

Password Recovery

Often, users will remember their usernames but not their passwords. Most sites have a link on the login page or near the username/password blanks that says something along the lines of "to reset password click here" or "forgot password? click here." When users click the link, they are taken to a password recovery form where they need to enter their username or email address. Then, the website in question will send them via email either (1) a new password or (2) a link they must click from their email to bring them back to the website in question to reset the password. These links include a token—or small piece of computer code—that verifies it has come from the email account in question. In this way, users can recover or reset a forgotten password using their email account.

Phishing

Phishing, when scammers send emails meant to deceive users by imitation legitimate communications from trusted sources, looks a lot like password recovery. Many phishing scams appear as emails from your bank or credit card companies, complete with realistic graphic design that emulates legitimate company email. These emails will often have a warning along the lines of "your credit account has been compromised!" or "your Facebook account has been hacked!" and will include a link to reset your password. These nefarious links work like a password recovery link, but with the remote Internet scammers gaining access to your account information.

COMMON PROBLEMS AND HOW TO SOLVE THEM

- Users might choose a username that is unavailable, and not understand why it is unavailable. Explain that these are like phone numbers, and so everyone needs their own. You can say something along the lines of "there are a lot of Becky Murphys out there, and another one got to your name first," and suggest ways to make the address unique.
- Users may have trouble still understanding the difference between email address and username, especially as it relates to usernames on different websites. They just need to hear it over and over again.

WORKSHOP PLAN

Introduction: Introduce yourself, and explain that this class covers usernames and logins, two of the most essential Internet skills to help with email accounts and with most other pages and services participants access online.

Remind participants that an email address is made up of two parts, a unique and personal username, and the domain name where the account has been registered. Understanding these two parts is crucial to convenient and private Internet browsing. The reason for this is that now most websites, from shopping to news and weather, encourage or require users to log on, using an email address, usually along with other information. In some cases, you can log onto a website using just your email address (e.g., Facebook, Google, or Microsoft accounts), but in many more cases, individual websites (and apps) require individual logins. These often take the form of (1) an email address, (2) a site-specific username, and (3) a password.

Explain to the class that they will practice signing up for a web service that requires a username and password, by registering on a common commenting service, disqus.com (pronounced like "discuss"). Disqus bills itself as the "web's community of communities," because it is a special website and piece of software code that adds comment functionality to any website. So if the library wanted to include a commenting feature on our catalogue, so patrons could comment on books and movies, it might pay Disqus for the right to integrate their software/website code into their catalogue website. That way, users could leave comments. Tell the participants that you will now register an account.

Navigate with your mouse to the upper right-hand side of the screen and click small white text that says "log in." The page will immediately change and present you with a login screen.

Type disqus.com in the URL bar and hit enter

Figure 3.1   Type disqus.com and hit "go" on your browser.

Standard login screen

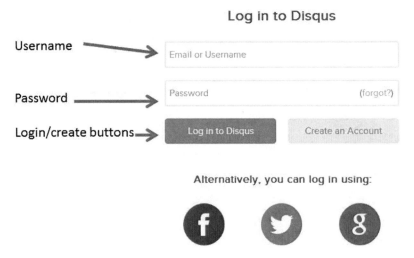

Figure 3.2   A typical login screen, with blanks for username and password, as well as a password reset link.

Show the class how Disqus offers other options for logging in. Users can log in to Disqus with their Facebook account information (the F graphic), Twitter account information (the bird graphic), or Google account information (the G graphic). Explain that this is a tempting option, because it is very convenient and they would be much less likely to forget their login information to one of these major web services (Facebook or Gmail especially) than you are to some smaller, individual service or website such as Disqus. Caution them to give careful consideration, though, noting that choosing this option gives their Facebook, Twitter, or Gmail login information to the Disqus service. While their terms of service will spell out privacy expectations and what they can do with the information they gather, users should beware that choosing this option often leads to things such as:

1. A website automatically emailing everyone in their email address book to invite them to join up
2. Disqus (or whatever website/service is being signed up for) posting a status update to their Facebook feed or automatically tweeting that they have joined up
3. All of their activity on a third-party site (such as Disqus) being made available in the metadata—how the ads are generated—of their email or Facebook

After this explanation, return to practicing sign up with new usernames. Click "Create an account."

Show the typical login screen in action, with blanks for (1) email address, (2) username, and (3) password.

Note that by filling out this form and signing up an account with Disqus, participants can (and should!) pick a password for Disqus that is different from their email passwords.

Ask the class to fill in their email addresses, and pick new usernames and passwords for Disqus. Mention that if any of them keeps a journal or day calendar, it is good to get in the habit of keeping track of various usernames and passwords they are using on various sites. Some Internet users prefer to keep this information in some sort of code, in case they lose their list.

Explain that as users sign up with different websites and services, they may encounter various username and password rules. These are not universal across the Internet. Rather, each website can set its own rules. Some rules might include whether capitalization (case) counts, how many characters a username may consist of, whether certain characters (e.g., a capital letter, a number, or some other symbol) must or may be used, and so on. Urge participants to read carefully. Sometimes these rules are stated up front on a particular service (but in small print), and others might not tell you what is required until you have entered something invalid first.

Explain that when picking a password, it's important to pick a "strong" password. Computerized password hackers are able to try hundreds of thousands of combinations of letters and numbers until they get something that works. Strong passwords are a user's best defense against computerized hacking. Strong passwords are hard-to-guess, appear to be a random collection of numbers, letters, because they are completely made up by you and cannot be found in any dictionary or automated list of words. Strong passwords also use punctuation, and can make use of uppercase and lowercase letters. Something like "bX57ut0p1A" is a lot harder to guess than "rover6284," for example.

Tell users that picking a strong password requires creative thinking. You want the end result to be something that looks completely random and would be hard to guess, but that you can easily remember. But how do you come up with something along the lines of "bX57ut0p1A" or "Mn1Da1fK"? The best method is to think about password phrases that are whole sentences, which can then be encoded.

For example, you might think up a passphrase such as "My name is Dorothy and I'm from Kansas." You could take the first letter of each word in the phrase and you would get "mnidaifk." Imagine, for a moment, that the website you are creating a password for requires that you use numbers and capital letters. You could use a common number-for-letter substitution such as 1 for I, 2 for T, 3 for E, 4 for A, 5 for F, 6 for G, 7 for K, 8 for H, 9 for N, and 0 for O, for example.

If you apply these number swaps and add in one capital letter to start the password and give a capital D for Dorothy and a capital K for Kansas, because they were capital letters in your original sentence, your passphrase

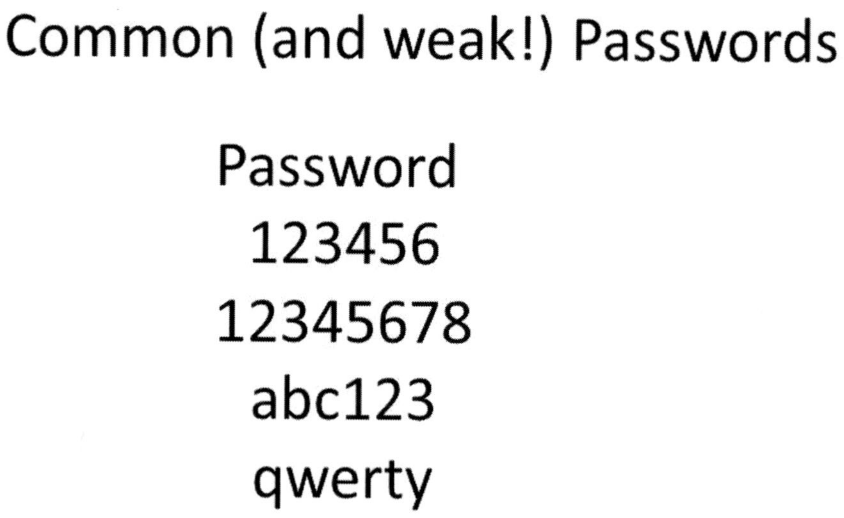

Common (and weak!) Passwords

Password
123456
12345678
abc123
qwerty

Figure 3.3   Users should avoid these common, weak passwords.

becomes "Mn1Da1fK." And while this seems completely random, you just need to remember your original sentence, and that you swapped numbers in.

Ask users to choose a phrase, and then turn it into a strong password. Have them use this password to sign up for Disqus.

Once they have created a password and signed up, they should be able to log in to their email accounts and see a message from Disqus confirming that they just signed up. Tell them to go ahead and log in to confirm that.

Explain that after you sign up for a website, it is customary to get a confirmation email. These sometimes ask the recipient to click a link to confirm that their email address is a real, working email address. If you have just signed up for a new website or service, these confirmation links are probably safe. But if an email like this appears out of nowhere, it may very well be an example of phishing.

Explain that phishing is a kind of Internet scam in which scammers send emails meant to deceive users by imitating emails that are safe or from trusted sources. Many phishing scams appear as emails from a recipient's bank or credit card companies, complete with realistic graphic design that emulates legitimate company email. These emails often contain a warning along the lines of "your credit account has been compromised!" or "your Facebook account has been hacked!" and include a link to reset your password. When the recipient clicks that link, though, he or she may be exposing their private account information to scammers (who use it for?). Beware of phishing!

HANDS-ON ACTIVITIES

A. Resetting password

Have the class practice resetting their email passwords. They can do this by traveling to their webmail account uniform resource locator (URL), and clicking "forgot password" to run through the steps to reset it. Tell them to expect lots of tiny problems to solve along the way!

B. Weak passwords into strong passwords

Ask participants to turn the following weak passwords into strong passwords:

12345

pass123

billy89

catscats

swinton

l1brary

C. Tell class to come up with systems for encoding their own strong passwords. This could include switching the order of the letters, using numbers for letters, or inserting punctuation. Starting with the following passphrases, create strong passwords:

My first cat was an orange tabby named Mango.

I rode Tram 20 once a week.

Once upon a time, Cinderella was my favorite story.

April is the cruelest month.

The capital city of Vermont is Montpelier, but the largest city is Burlington.

I have had a library card since first grade.

I learned to swim at the YMCA on Chestnut Street.

My aunt and uncle live around the corner.

Octavia Butler and Gloria Naylor are two of my favorite writers.

Into the Woods is not my favorite musical.

4

Typing and Documents

This workshop shows users the basics of using a word processing program and using a keyboard to enter text. In it, they create and save documents and experiment with style and font. It should be conducted as at least a one-hour workshop for the basics, with more one-hour workshops to finish and polish a resume or cover letter. *Note:* Because resumes are so format-intensive, it is best to start with a cover letter and save the resume for an additional workshop (or for a longer workshop). If you are time limited and cannot offer an extra resume section, practice formatting and spacing/tabbing in the cover letter for maximum benefit to a user looking to compose a resume after.

AFTER-CLASS COMPETENCIES

After this workshop, users should be able to:

- Use the keyboards to input numbers, letters, punctuation, and other symbols
- Format text size, font face, page spacing, and more in a document
- Create a text document using Microsoft Word, Google Documents, or other word processing program
- Draft, save, and attach a resume or cover letter to an email

BEFORE CLASS

- Pull sample resumes from books in your library collection, or print out a sample resume from an online source such as http://obamacto.org/ or http://www.gcflearnfree.org/resumewriting/extra/2. (The latter source, GCFLearn-Free (www.gcflearnfree.org) is a free online learning resource to bookmark for many uses!)
- Pull sample cover letters, personal letters, or business letters from your collection, as well, as samples. Depending on your user group, you may want to

generate a small sample text yourself for everyone to practice typing. (It does not have to be a letter.)

- Figure out whether users will be able to save to a library computer (at least temporarily), or if they will need a flash drive in order to save documents during this workshop. If they need a flash drive, be sure to advertise that ahead of time or have several available for practice.

KEY CONCEPTS

The following *key concepts* are presented to learners in the training script, slides, and hands-on activities. Familiarize yourself with them and refer back to this list as needed.

Word Processing Software and Apps

Word processing software and apps are special kinds of software that let users compose and work with text. There are many different word processing programs and apps on the market, but the most common is Microsoft Word. You will probably be using Word, as it is known colloquially, in these lessons. A second and increasingly common word processing program is actually a web app from Google called Google Drive. Actually, its appearance and core functionality are modeled after Microsoft Word, and users will find that the skills learned in one readily transfer to the other. One major difference is that Google Drive stores all of a user's documents online ("in the cloud"), whereas Microsoft Word's storage and retrieval model is desktop/physical location one. Users will need to save Microsoft Word documents to a computer hard drive or portable Universal Serial Bus (USB) drive. Note that Microsoft also now has a corresponding cloud-based service for storing documents as well called SkyDrive. Beyond these two main competitors, there are many others: generic text editors such a Notepad or Textedit, a proprietary Apple program called Pages that works on iOS devices and Macs, open-source and free applications such as Open Office, and many others.

Documents

When you use a computer to type information and want to save that text and information to later retrieval, to attach to email to send someone, or print out, you are generating a file called a document. The most common form of computer document is a file with the extension .docx, and it is the most common because that is standard Microsoft Word format. Google Drive, iOS, and MacOS Pages and other word processing software has conversion options to and from .docx file format built-in. Users must create new blank documents when they begin using a word processor. In Google

(Free) Alternatives to Microsoft Word and Alternatives to Google Drive

Open Office (Openoffice.org)—leading open-source version of word processing, as well as other open-source products that emulate the rest of the Microsoft Office suite (e.g., Excel, PowerPoint)

LibreOffice (libreoffice.org)—another leading open-source version of Microsoft Office analogues.

AbiWord (Abisource.com)—an open-source program that runs on many different operating systems (Unix, Windows, MacOS, etc.) and is highly customizable via free download plugins.

NeoOffice (http://www.neooffice.org)—a program designed to emulate Microsoft Office for MacOS.

Zoho (http://www.zoho.com/) is a browser-based web tool with a word processing application as well as other productivity software.

Drive, there is an option under the file menu to "create new document." In Microsoft Word, users must click on the "Office button," a four-color blinking button in the upper left-hand corner of the program window and then select "New."

Save vs. Save As

Users of desktop word processors such as Microsoft Word should learn to save their work early and often to avoid losing any typing; and also to practice giving documents names and putting them in locations that make them easy to retrieve for editing and attaching later. Save just saves the current information in the file at its present location. This can be problematic, especially for users on a public PC, because the current location might be a downloads folder, or a temporary location buried deep in a file directory that will be difficult to find later. So "Save as" becomes a better choice, because it forces users to confirm (and allows users to change) three attributes about the file:

1. The name
2. The location
3. The file format (*Note:* See later for more on file formats and types.)

Important Keys

Most of the keys on the keyboard correspond to letters or numbers, and are easy for inexperienced beginners to figure out. But there are few abstract or counterintuitive keys that are crucial to point out and explain

- Backspace: This key deletes text letter by letter from the right to the left. So, if someone wants to erase the last letter they typed, they use Backspace.
- Delete: This key deletes text letter by letter from left to right. Use this key when you are editing or when you are deleted large amounts of text at once.
- Enter or Return: Located on the right-hand side of the keyboard, usually the last letter in the row that begins ASDF, this key brings the cursor down a line in the page, and is the key a user should strike when they want to begin a new paragraph. (*Note:* When using web forms, that is, filling out forms, applications, or billing information online, this key often has the functionality of clicking "Next," "Done," or "Finish" at the end of the page. If users hit it prematurely by accident, the page will attempt to save the work displayed and move to the next page, just as if a user had clicked the link.)
- Spacebar: This key creates a blank space between words.
- Shift: On most keyboards there are two of these keys, one on each side of the keyboard, for convenience. In the case of letters, holding down the Shift key while striking a letter types the uppercase letter. For number or punctuation mark keys, holding down the Shift key while you strike a number of punctuation key types the symbol on the top half of the key.
- Tab: This key adds one tab (about five blank spaces) to a line of text. It is most often used to indent a paragraph.

View and Zoom

Users can enlarge the view of their documents by adjusting the zoom (zooming in or zooming out). This feature is useful for seniors, young people, and users with vision limitations. It does not change the size of the words in the file (i.e., they would not print enlarged, or be viewed enlarged if opened via email attachment on another computer). Change these options by looking for a "View" menu and selecting "Zoom" in Microsoft Word or another layout in Google Drive. (*Note:* Because Google Drive is a browser-based web tool, the keyboard shortcut for increasing the text size (zooming in) discussed in a previous chapter works here, too: hold down Ctrl and Shift while striking the + symbol key to zoom in (make the text bigger); hold down Ctrl while striking the—symbol key to zoom out (make the text smaller).)

Font and Font Size

Word processing programs let users pick what they want their text to look like and are highly customizable. One of the ways users customize text is by changing the font or typeface or the size. Most word processing programs come with various styles to choose from, and there are thousands of fonts available for download and use. Microsoft Word has more than 100 preinstalled; Google Drive comes with a more modest 16 on its main menu, but users can quickly access hundreds more. In addition, users can change the size of their text. Size is measured in points, and can be set to any point from 1 to 1638. "Normal" printed text is usually between 10 and 14 points.

Bold, Italic, and Underline

Three other basic and standard text formatting options exist, and should already be familiar to even a beginning user. They are:

1. Bold
2. Italic
3. Underline

In both Google Drive and Microsoft Word (as well as most others), users can select these options from a toolbar across the top of the screen. Once a user clicks the *B* for bold, the *I* for italics, or the *U* for underlining, the next letters typed will appear in that style. Alternatively, users can compose everything in regular type, highlight and select text (see later), and then click these formatting buttons. These effects can be combined, for *bold underlining*, or *bold italics*, or *even all three at once*!

Document Settings

When users want the same styles to apply to their entire text, or they want to modify attributes such as line spacing, space between paragraphs, size of margins, and so on, they will access the document settings or formatting settings. In Microsoft Word, these are called document settings and are found under the page layout menu. In Google Drive, they are under the format menu. In both of these word processing programs, there are also paragraph styles and settings to explore. In general, beginning users will only want to modify the text between single spaced (appropriate for a letter) or double spaced (appropriate for a school or college paper).

Selecting Text, Copying, and Pasting

Being able to copy some text from a website or from another document (or another section of your document) and paste it elsewhere represents one of the major innovations computerized word processing differs from old-fashioned typewriters. First, users must highlight or select the text they seek to copy. To highlight, users should hover the cursor in front of or behind the text they want to copy. Then they should click the house button and hold down the left-click button. While holding down the button, users can drag the cursor up and down, right and left to until the text they want to select is highlighted, or surrounded by a shading. This highlighting and selecting can be tricky for beginning—and even seasoned—mouse users. As with any computer task, there are various ways of achieving copy and paste. The three most common and useful are:

- Right-click option: Once your text is highlighted, place the cursor over any part of the highlighted text and click the right mouse button. This right-click accesses a menu of options. Click "Copy" (using the left mouse button). Then click where you want to insert the pasted text. Right-click again, and select "Paste" with the left button.

- Keyboard shortcuts: With text highlighted, hold down the Ctrl key and strike the "C" key. (This copies the highlighted text. No action or animation appears on the screen when this happens.) Then, holding down Ctrl again while striking the "V" key will paste.

- Using file menus: In Google Drive and in older versions of Microsoft Word, with text highlighted, click the "Edit" menu and then select copy/paste from that menu.

Line Spacing

In documents, "line spacing" refers to the amount of whitespace in between lines of text. There are many options, but the most common are "single," "1.5," and "double." Single spacing fits more text on one page, but the lines are closer together. Double spacing is appropriate for things like school essays or manuscripts because it puts a whole extra line of whitespace between lines of text, which makes it easier to read, and to make comments. Documents may automatically start out single spaced, but users can change that setting at any point. If users change it after they have already typed part of the document, they should select or highlight the entire text and then apply these spacing changes. Users can right-click on highlighted text, then select "paragraph options" in Microsoft Word, or look for the "line spacing" option under the format file menu in Google Drive.

Justification

In documents, text is justified to the left, to the center, or to the right, which means that the edge of the text is lined up against the right side of the page, the left side of the page or down the middle. Centering is often used for titles, and right justification sometimes for addresses or headings. Left-side justification is usually the default. (Full justification means the text is stretched to line up on both left and right sides of the page.)

Document File Types

There are almost as many file types as there are kinds of computer or tablet or smartphone, and sometimes users have trouble understanding when to use which one. As discussed in the section on documents earlier, the most common form is Microsoft's proprietary format, the .docx (or on older versions of Microsoft Word, .doc). Other file types that users will encounter in word processing programs include the following:

- .rtf, or rich-text format: These are plain and generic text files that can be opened by a variety of different word processing files. They do not feature rich formatting options, and are perfect for someone sending a file when they are not sure exactly how the person they are sending it to will open it.

- .txt, for text file: This is another plain text file with no formatting. These can be hard for users to work with because they often do not feature automatic text wraparound at the end of line.

- .pdf, or portable document format: This file type is a proprietary but standard way of sending "frozen" documents, or ones not able to be edited. Because all word processors format files differently based on system defaults, any .rtf or .docx might not display the way a user intended on a different machine or when printed out. Using .pdf format ensures that your document is saved and later displayed in exactly the format a user intended. (*Note:* For advanced users, note that there are some .pdfs with editable fields meant to be filled out and saved. These are often forms, so the form blanks will be editable but the rest of the text will not be. Note also that any .pdf will be editable using the proprietary Adobe Professional application.)

Spell Check and Grammar Check

Most word processing programs include a spelling and/or grammar checking tool. Users should look for it under the review menu in Microsoft Word, or under the tools menu in Google Drive. It is sometimes represented in these programs with a checkmark and the letters ABC on an icon. In addition, Microsoft Word and Google Drive both check spelling as you type, offering a display-only red squiggly line underneath any words it thinks are spelled incorrectly. In addition, Microsoft Word points out what it considers infelicitous grammar with a green squiggly underline. In both cases—for spelling and for grammar where available—the programs are using a predefined dictionary of words or concepts that might not encompass the words someone is using, or suggest that slang is spelled incorrectly. While spell check can be a useful tool for users, keep in mind that these programs are checking a specific dictionary that might not include the needed words. (*Note:* Advanced users can add words to the dictionary in Microsoft Word, which might be handy for certain proper nouns or other frequently used jargon.)

COMMON PROBLEMS AND HOW TO SOLVE THEM

- These instructions refer to the most current versions of Microsoft Word (2010) running on a PC. If you are using an older version, or a Mac, some of the menus and buttons will be in different places. Note, though, that the core functionality has not changed, and that these menus and options are available in older versions. Familiarize yourself with your version of Microsoft Word before class and compare its menus to the ones described here. Adjust as necessary.

- If using Google Documents, users might need extra time or assistance in logging in or authenticating their account on the library computer. This could eat up valuable time and increase participant frustration before the workshop has even started. Consider introducing Google Documents near the end for more advanced users, if you have access to another word processing software.

- Be sure the view/magnification is appropriate to your user base, and that you have adjusted the zoom by navigating to view->zoom, so users are not forced to type in a very large font size to see their document clearly.

WORKSHOP PLAN

Introduction: Introduce yourself and explain that in this class participants will learn about typing documents in a word processing program. Explain that the first step is to work in one word processing program, Microsoft Word, but let participants know that if have questions about other ways to type documents or have used other software programs, they should let you know.

Explain that word processing programs let computer users type and edit documents. They also let you print documents. Using Microsoft Word, you can make everything from a flyer to business cards, calendars to forms. Tell participants that in this class, they will practice the basic skills they need to type almost anything.

Demonstrate how to double click the icon to open Microsoft Word, and point out the menu at the top of the screen.

Note: Depending on your version of Microsoft Word and your operating system, these menus may look different.

Tell users that most word processors open to a new, blank document that looks like a blank white page, with a blinking cursor. Have participants try hitting any letter or number key, and notice how it appears on the screen. If it doesn't, show users how to create a new document.

Typical Microsoft Word Menus

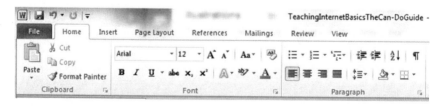

Figure 4.1   Here is a typical view of the menu options available in a current version of Microsoft Word.

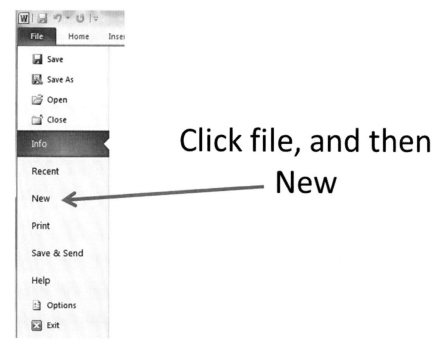

Figure 4.2   Click New document to create a new, blank document.

Explain that everything on the blank screen is the document. Participants in the class will add to the document by typing words or numbers in this class, but let them know that a finished document could have pictures, graphs, or other images, too. Tell them they will also spend a lot of time experimenting with these documents before anything is final, and practice changing the size of the words, the style of the text, the spacing, and so on. First though, they will learn to save the document. That way, in case they accidentally close a window or your computer freezes, they will be able to reopen your document.

Note: If you are in Google Drive, documents save automatically and you can disregard this step. In Microsoft Sky Drive, there is only a "Save as" option, so there is no need to distinguish between "Save" and "Save as," as there is for users using desktop copies of Microsoft Word.

Explain that this file has been saved with a name, that is to say, the mostly blank document has been saved as the file "Sample1.doc."

Show the participants how to save as they go along, by just clicking File Save. If they want to change the name of the document, from say "Sample1" to "Resume2015," for example, they would have to click "Save as" again.

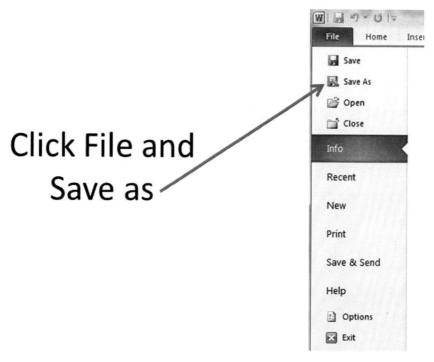

Click File and Save as

Figure 4.3 Type a file name such as "Sample1" and hit enter. Use the Save as option to double check where you are saving the file.

Tell your class that "Save as" is a powerful option because it lets users control three things about every file. The three attributes are:

1. The name of the file
2. The location of the file (which folder on your local hard drive, a flash or zip drive, or a web-based file saving service such as Dropbox, for example)
3. The file format. This option is especially useful if you are need a format other than the default file format for your word processing program, which in this case is .doc (Microsoft Word document).

So far, the class has mostly used the mouse to interact with the computer. Now, participants are going to start using the keyboard to input text, numbers, and punctuation. Most keys only have one symbol on them. For a lowercase letter, strike the key you want. For an uppercase letter, hold down Shift and then strike the key you want. Ask participants to locate the Shift key; and tell them it's one of the most important keys. Now, note that some keys have two symbols on them, one at the bottom of the key and on at the top. Shift is what lets you access the symbols along the tops of the keys. So, they can strike 2 for 2, but should hold down Shift and strike 2 for @.

Most important keys:
BACKSPACE, DELETE, ENTER or RETURN

TAB, SHIFT and SPACEBAR

Figure 4.4   The most important and useful keys for a beginning computer user to learn.

Explain to the class that they will now look at some other keys on their keyboard that are as important as Shift. Instruct them to look at their keyboards as you talk and find the keys you're referring to.

Backspace deletes text letter by letter from the right to the left. To erase the last thing you typed, they use Backspace. This key is often confused with the Delete key, which deletes text letter by letter from left to right. The only difference is the direction in which the cursor moves to delete.

Enter or *Return*, located on the right-hand side of the keyboard, is usually the last letter in the row that begins ASDF. This key is referred to as Enter or Return interchangeably. This key brings the cursor down a line in the page, and is the key you should strike to start a new paragraph.

Spacebar, at the bottom of the keyboard in the center, is this key creates a blank space between words.

Shift was already covered, but remember that it does not matter which Shift key you use, and that there are two to make them easier to hit on either side of the keyboard as you type. In the case of letters, holding down the Shift key while striking a letter types the uppercase letter. For number or punctuation mark keys, holding down the Shift key while you strike a number of punctuation key types the symbol on the top half of the key.

The last important key to look at for word processing is the *Tab* key, which adds one tab (about five blank spaces) in front of a line of text. It is most often used to indent a paragraph.

Sample text

And then Donna said to everybody for the 10th time, "Quiet down!"

Figure 4.5   Use a sample sentence such as this one for users to practice typing and then formatting text.

Have users practice typing the earlier sentence, exactly as they see it (as displayed in Figure 4.5): And then Donna said to everybody for the 10th time, "Quiet down!"

In this sentence, all of the important keys discussed earlier are used, except the tab key. If you were writing this as the beginning of a new paragraph, you could also start with a tab.

Have the class keep practicing by deleting a couple symbols or letters and retyping them. When everyone has this sentence in their document, you're ready to take the next steps.

Tell participants that now they will learn how to enlarge text. For example, they may want to format the name and address in a big, noticeable headline typeface at the top of their resumes, with the rest of information about education and experience in a standard 10- or 12-point font. Font refers to how big the text will be *when it is printed out on paper*. Emphasize to the class that it is important to not confuse that with the size of the text on the screen. You might have poor eyesight and want a zoomed-in view, or you might have excellent eyesight and want to see more of your document at the same time, so you could zoom out. The way to change your view of the text on the screen is to use the *view* or *zoom* options built into the word processing program. In Microsoft Word, there is a view tab at the top. Click it to see all the view options.

You will see many options, but the most important of which are:

- Print layout
- Full screen reading

- Web layout
- Outline
- Draft
- Zoom

Note: All of these options *simply adjust the way your text and document appear on the screen*. They do not affect how the document would look when it is printed.

Encourage participants to click through all of these options to see what they do to the view, but draw their attention to the following:

Print layout: This is how the document will look on a page. Typically, the paper page is represented by white space, and then outside of the page the screen will be gray.

Full screen reading: This stretches your document text to fill the entire screen, so you can write or edit without distractions on the screen.

Zoom: This option opens up a dialogue box with yet more options. It can be overwhelming at first, but is fairly simple once you get used to it. The most important things in this box are the percentages listed. If your text was displaying too small and you want to zoom in, increase the percentage (maybe from 100% to 120% or 150%, etc.). If your text was displaying too big and you wanted to zoom out, reduce the percentage by 10 or 20 percent and you will see that the text appears smaller.

This is a good time to explain to the class that sometimes all of the toolbars and options can get confusing. Tell them that you will show them special keyboard shortcuts that do the same job much more quickly and with few or no clicks of the mouse at all. For zooming in and out in Microsoft Word (as well as in Internet browsers), there is a convenient keyboard shortcut that was covered in a previous session or workshop. To make type appear bigger: hold down Ctrl and Shift while striking the + symbol key; hold down Ctrl while striking the—symbol key to zoom out (make the text appear smaller). Have your students practice with this method until the view is the right size for them.

Mention that if you are using a computer mouse with a wheel, you can zoom in and zoom out by holding down the Ctrl key while wheeling the wheel away from you to zoom in and toward you to zoom out.

Tell the class that they are now going to learn how to manipulate the size and shape of letters with font size and style. Explain that *font* means typeface, or the style of the letters. Point out that near the top left of the menu, they will see the name of the current font in a dropdown box. It probably says "Calibri" or "Times New Roman" or "Cambria" right now. Explain that those are the default fonts in Microsoft Word and Google Drive, which means they are the ones that are turned on when a user starts typing.

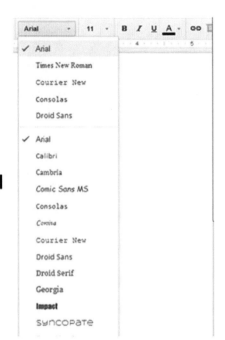

Use the Font drop down menu to select a new typeface

Figure 4.6   Use the drop down menus in a word processing program to select a new font or typeface style.

Tell users to choose a font style, and then ask them to type the sample sentence again: And then Donna said to everybody for the 10th time, "Quiet down!"

Point out that users can also change the size of the type. "Normal" printed text is usually somewhere between 10 and 14 points. The bigger the number, the larger the letters. Note that letters can be formatted to be really gigantic—too big to even fit on one printed page. The minimum point size is 1, which is probably too tiny to see with the naked eye, and the maximum point size is 1638. Ask students to click in the font size drop-down menu to the right of the font name, and select a new number.

Now have the class type the sample sentence again, in a bigger font: And then Donna said to everybody for the 10th time, "Quiet down!"

Explain that to the class will now learn three more options for adding different styles to the typed words. These are *italics*, *bold*, and *underline*. To achieve these effects, users should bring their cursors to the bar at the top of their screen, and click the *B* for bold, the *I* for italics, or the *U* for underlining. After they click each button, the next letters typed will appear in that style. Note that these effects can be combined, for *bold underlining*, or *bold italics*, or *even all three at once*!

Have the class practice using these three styles.

Typing the same sentence over and over again is good practice, but tell users you will now show them an even easier way to achieve these effects: that is, by copying the first sentence and then pasting it again with a new style.

Explain that to copy and paste, users first need to learn to select text. That means that highlighting it by using the mouse. To highlight, or select, text, tell them to hold the mouse cursor at the beginning of the line(s) they want to select. Then click once and hold down the button. Ask them to keep the mouse button depressed as they drag the cursor right to select the text in question. As users drag their cursors, they will see that text is now surrounded by a blue or black highlight or shadow effect. Note that the default color is usually blue, but that it may appear in any color based on PC settings. This highlighting means that the text has been selected, and while it is selected, users can change the font, font size, or make the text bold, italicized, or underlined.

Show users/Slide content: With text selected, change the:

- Font
- Font size
- Turn on bold
- Turn on italics
- Turn on underline

Tell the class that another thing they can do with selected (or highlighted) text is to copy and paste it. Remind them that computers can do the exact same thing multiple ways. Tell participants that they are going to learn three different ways of copying and pasting selected text, and everyone should figure out which is the best and most comfortable for them.

First, ask them highlight the text they want to copy.

Option 1 is the *right-click* option: place the cursor over any part of the highlighted text and click the right mouse button. This right-click accesses a menu of options. Click "Copy" (using the left mouse button). Then click where you want to insert the pasted text. Right-click again, and select "Paste" with the left button.

Option 2 is *keyboard shortcuts*. Hold down the Ctrl key and strike the "C" key. This copies the highlighted text. Note that no action or animation appears on the screen when this happens. Then, placing the cursor on the page where you'd like the text to appear, hold down the Ctrl key again, and strike the "V" key. This will paste the text. Remind users that they just learned the zoom in/zoom out keyboard shortcuts.

Tell users: Option 3, using the *file menus*, also works. In Google Drive and in older versions of Microsoft Word, with text highlighted, click the "Edit" menu and then select copy/paste from that menu.

Tell users that keyboard shortcuts are powerful and useful because they are usually effective across multiple different software applications. That means that what works in Microsoft Word (or the word processing program of your choice) will also work in an Internet browser or other software.

This is also a great time to tell users about the "Undo" shortcut, which also works across a variety of programs. This command simply undoes the last thing a user typed or did, so it is useful in case you accidentally deleted a whole document by clicking in the wrong place. The "Undo" command is Ctrl + Z, so hold down the Ctrl key and strike "Z." Ask the class to practice undoing some of the pasting they just did.

Tell class that they now have more time to practice what they have already learned and find out what more they want to know. Take a few last questions related to anything in the workshop, then transition to a series of hands-on activities that will help users practice their new skills.

HANDS-ON ACTIVITIES

A. Resume. Pass out the resume sample or books from your resume collection to use.

- Using the sample resumes provided, have class members type up their own. The goal is to get at least a draft, and to save it for later use.

B. Cover letter. Pass out the sample cover letter or appropriate book from your collection to use as a sample.

- Using the sample cover letter provided, ask participants to type up their own. The goal is to get at least a draft, and to save it for later use. *Note:* If users are not interested in writing a cover letter or are not job seekers, encourage them to write a letter to a friend or family member who lives far away. Yet a third option that will captivate some users is for them to write a complaint letter about a product or service.

- After they have several lines of text, encourage students to experiment with the spacing. Tell them to highlight the text, and then use the right-click to open up "paragraph options." Direct them to switch between single spaced (1), one and a half spaced (1.5), or double spaced (2). In each case, the spacing refers to how much space there is in between each horizontal line of text in your document.

C. Attachments

- Ask users to identify one of the documents they have been working on that they would like to attach to an email.
- Direct them to "Save as" so they can (1) save their document, (2) see where they are saving it, and (3) give it a new name if necessary.
- Direct users to log in to their email. Users without email accounts should be directed to sign up for one. They probably do not have enough time to sign up for an account and to practice attachments today.

- Tell users to compose a new email message, and to put their email address in the "to" field. They will be sending their resume or other document to themselves.
- Ask users to look for the attachment button, which will either say "Attach" or look like a paperclip. When they click "Attach" or the paper-clip button, a dialogue box appears where they can browse for and select their file. Show them how to find it (recalling from "Save as" that they saved it either on the desktop of the library computer, or in the documents folder, or perhaps on their own flash drive), and then click on it to select it. Note that some email programs may require an additional click to actually attach the document to the email, and some will attach directly from the dialogue box.
- The last step is for users to actually send (and receive!) the email with their document attached.

D. For advanced users. Direct users to save their documents as a PDF file. This file format, which stands for portable document format, is useful for sending documents that have specific or special formatting. This file format lets users control how their document is viewed on a different computer or device. The .doc (Microsoft Word document) format does not offer users that control.

- Direct users to click "Save as."
- Click on the "type" dropdown menu, and select PDF.
- *Note*: In older versions of Microsoft Word (anything pre-2007), this option is located under the Print menu Save as PDF, not under the "Save as" menu.
- In Google Drive, click file, then mouse over "Download as" and select PDF. This will download a PDF version of the document.

5

Introduction to Internet Search

This workshop is easily taught in one hour. Spend 20 minutes at the end letting users search for their own interests, and help them find relevant and authoritative pages to look at. This workshop can also be repurposed as an information literacy workshop/research orientation for teens.

AFTER-CLASS COMPETENCIES

After this workshop, users should be able to:

- Perform basic and advanced searches using Google or another search engine
- Search for text results, visual/photographic results, or video results
- Recognize "junk" websites or link farms
- Assess the credibility of a given web page
- Narrow search results in a search engine by using more keywords or limiting options until the results are the most relevant
- Use Twitter, Facebook, or Instagram to search a particular hashtag
- Understand why search results are in a particular order

KEY CONCEPTS

The following *key concepts* are presented to learners in the training script, slides, and hands-on activities. Familiarize yourself with them and refer back to this list as needed.

Credibility

The Internet is so diverse and powerful precisely because anyone can contribute content and information on web pages, blogs, or message boards.

As a result, though, there is very little authority control. This can result in (1) inaccurate information or (2) unverified information. Users learning to search online need to be introduced to the concept of credibility, and should learn how to be prepared to find and recognize trusted sources.

Search Engines

Search engines are special websites made for searching for other websites. By far, the most well known is Google. A second runner-up is Yahoo. (Other search engines include Bing, Ask, Webcrawler, and many more.) Search engines send automated computer programs (called robots) all over the Internet, reading and indexing pages. Based on the actual text websites display, as well as on special text and information web designers code invisibly into pages, these robots decide what the site is "about" and whether the content matches what a given user has search for. Whatever a user inputs into the search field is called a "query." Different search engines rely on different methods to make sure that the websites/links they are delivering are relevant to the original query. One method is the number of clicks a link gets: the more users who click to a website, the more relevant this site seems to a search engine like Google. This is important because it means that some search results will appear near the top of the list, even if they are not relevant!

Note: Visit www.thesearchenginelist.co/ for links to and annotations about more than 100 search engines, sorted by category.

Wikipedia and "Wikis"

Wikipedia is one of the most commonly accessed websites, and it is built on a collaborative platform called a "wiki." This collaborative platform means that the website is open to be edited by anyone. This does not mean that the content on Wikipedia is automatically suspect: Wikipedia has an editorial process and edits are tracked and vetted. However, sometimes misinformation or misleading information is introduced. Wikipedia is a fantastic tool for users wanting a quick overview of a given subject. Be sure to show your class how to follow the article references at the end of the article to verify the information, as well as learn more.

Directories

Directories, another special kind of web page, list links to other web pages based on the subject. They differ from search engines in that, rather than being categorized based on keywords and text matches, they are sorted instead by subject or category. The big search engine Yahoo used to function entirely as a directory, for example, offering users subject categories with many subheadings as a way to find other web pages. These directories can be powerful, because instead of being indexed by automated computer programs, the sites are instead categorized by human subject specialists. Two great examples are the Open Directory Project (http://www.dmoz.org) and the Internet Public Library (http://www.ipl.org/). Many users appreciate these web directories because the information has often been vetted by human subject specialists and as a result can include more trustworthy information.

Deep Web or Hidden Web

Search engines scan the text of web pages, looking for and indexing keywords. But a lot of the content of the Internet lurks below the surface, much of it in databases. These databases are full of information that, when queried, serve up dynamic web pages to Internet users. This is important because it means that there are millions of web pages that virtually *do not exist* until a user is looking for them. The pages themselves are literally created because of a particular search. All of this "hidden" or "deep" information is invisible to search engines (such as Google), that just crawl over the surface, looking for already established pages. But there are special search engines that allow users to search the deep web, and advanced users should know about these powerful options. Some examples include Clusty (clusty.com) or SurfWax (http://lookahead.surf wax.com/index-2011.html).

Hashtags on Twitter, Facebook, and Instagram

A relatively new way of finding information based on subject has emerged on Twitter and Facebook, and to a lesser extent Instagram. When people post Facebook status updates or send tweets, they often include a subject term marked with a hashtag (#). Then, users can search all of Twitter, for example, for other tweets that have that same hashtag. One excellent example might be a national (or international) televised awards show such as the Academy Awards. Users watching the show might "tag" their posts #Oscars or #Oscars2015, which lets them connect to any other person watching the show and tweeting about it. If someone were looking for crowd-generated information and content about the 2015 Academy Awards, the most effective way is to look at Facebook, Twitter, and Instagram posts with those same hashtags. This functionality need not be contained to one, televised event: tags like #campaign2016 or #gaymarriage are going to stay useful and relevant over a number of weeks, months, or years, and will lead users to posts tagged that way.

Social Search

While hashtags on Facebook and Twitter represent one form of powerful social searching, there are also other tools that Internet users can use to find out what their friends and communities online are saying or do know about a particular issue. These search tools give more credence to a particular website based on whether it has been used or mentioned on social networking sites. So the more something is posted in your and your friends' social media feeds, as well as across platforms such as Facebook or Twitter, the higher and more relevant that post or link will appear via social searches. Facebook Graph search is one example. In some ways, Google itself operates on social search principles in that, the more a given link is clicked and accessed, the more relevant it becomes to the search engine, and the higher it will appear in the search results. We can expect social search tools to become more and more useful and widespread as more people using the Internet link their Internet activities to their social media services.

COMMON PROBLEMS AND HOW TO SOLVE THEM

This workshop is usually pretty pitfall free. Most users are already used to the idea that there is a lot to find online, even if they don't have much experience looking for it. The most important error to watch out for is clicking on sponsored links (ads) instead of search results.

WORKSHOP PLAN

Introduce yourself and let the participants know that you are going to teach them about searching online.

Tell the class that there are billions of pages of websites on the Internet.[1] That's millions upon millions of pages with text, pictures, and other content that you can access. Obviously, just browsing for what you want would take forever, even if it were possible. How could you browse 10,000 pages looking for the right one, for example? So instead, as already mentioned in earlier sessions or workshops, you can get around the Internet more effectively by searching for the pages, sites, and content that you want. Explain that there are special kinds of websites called search engines whose job it is to "read" or "scan" web pages and then try to find them again based on the words they "read." The most famous search engine is Google. Another thing to note is that, according to Google, about 25 to 30 percent of the Internet is simply a bad copy of another web page.[2] So within that half billion pages, only about 75 percent is original. You might be wondering why there is so much copied junk online. The first reason is that it's easy to do—electronic texts and pictures are easily copied and republished. The second reason is that most of this "junk" publishing is done by computer programs automatically, and does not involve live humans.

These junk copies are meant to be filler. Companies pay advertisers when an Internet user clicks on their link, even if the user does not ultimately make any purchases. So Internet companies and advertisers public millions of pages of junk content with live links, hoping that users will click and that they will earn revenue. To increase their chances of revenue, they put copies of their ads (embedded in these junk web pages) everywhere. These kinds of websites are often called link farms. They look like real websites, they behave like real websites, and they have live links as real websites do, but if you scratch the surface, you can see that they are not legitimate. Explain that a link farm is a website or group of websites whose only purpose is to link to themselves. The more links, the more it seems legitimate to search engine robots or other ranking machines.

Caution users to watch out for websites that are junk! The best way to identify them is by being more familiar with the web. Other things you can watch out for:

- Blocks of text separated by big text links that seem unrelated to either the content on the page or the content you are looking for.
- Ad links that are designed to look like the navigation links on a page, that is, you think you are delving more deeply into a website but you are actually clicking on a sponsored ad and traveling via that linked ad to another site.
- Text and graphic ads that promise any kind of giveaway or sweepstakes. These fake contests often promise users a free iPad or laptop computer.
- Text that seems, for the first few lines, relevant to what you are looking for. When you read a couple paragraphs deeper, the content is usually revealed to be vague, unattributed to any author or source, or amateurishly written. This kind of junk website will also be filled with ads.

Instruct the class that they are going to learn about searching by practicing searching one search engine, Google. Remember, Google is a private, for-profit company that makes money off Internet users by offering services like free email and web searching that exposes Internet users to advertising. This might seem like a relatively simple point, but users need to keep it in mind as they search. So, Google's mission is not necessarily to serve up the best, most accurate, and current information for a given search—its mission is to make money through advertisements. Its search algorithms are designed to find and serve up web pages that an Internet user is most likely to click on or be looking for. This is a key difference you must remember as you search.

Show users: Click on the address bar and type: google.com.

Note: if you are using the Chrome browser, be sure to remind the class that the address bar is also a Google search bar.

Let students know that they will mostly be searching by using keywords. These are any word or phrase related to what you are searching for. The more you string together, the more specific your search will be.

Whenever searching, users should make a search string out a series of keywords about whatever it is they are looking for.

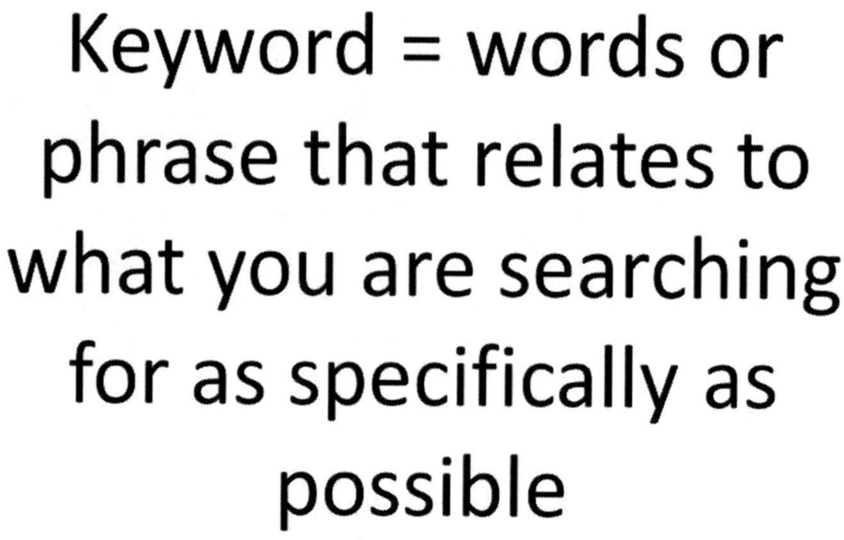

Keyword = words or phrase that relates to what you are searching for as specifically as possible

Figure 5.1   Keywords are words or phrase that specifically relate to what you are searching. Be as precise as possible for best results.

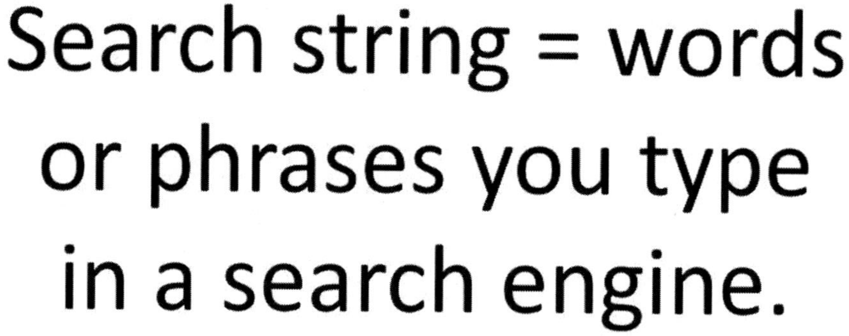

Search string = words or phrases you type in a search engine.

Figure 5.2   A search string—or query—is the words or phrases you use in a search engine.

Explain that the class is going to search for some general information. First, they'll search for information about the PrimetimeEmmys. Ask them to type "primetimeemmys" (without the quotation marks) into the search bar and press enter.

Spend a few minutes with participants looking at this search results page. There are a number of things you should point out to the class. The first thing to notice is that the search results page is color coded. The title of the page is in blue text and is underlined. Remember, that means it is a link

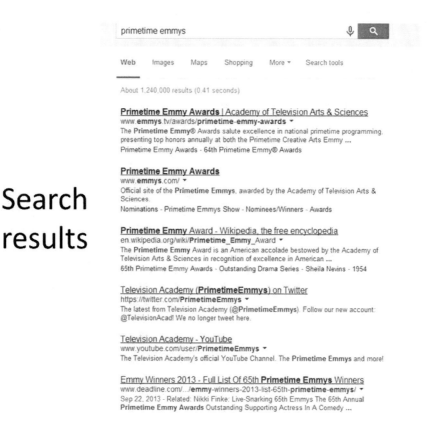

Search results

Figure 5.3 A page of Google results looks like this. Each has the link, the URL of the site, and a brief preview of the text on the site.

you can click on. Under the title, you will see the uniform resource locator (URL) or web address in green text. This is useful because users can make sure the title and the address match, or seem to match. If there is a discrepancy, you might be looking at a junk search result. Finally, there is black text that gives a description of the page or a preview of the text on the page.

1. Primetime Emmy Awards, with a URL of *emmys.tv*: This one seems to be the official site of Academy of Television Arts & Sciences that describes the Emmys.
2. Television Academy (PrimetimeEmmys) on Twitter, with a URL of twitter .com/PrimetimeEmmys: This is the official twitter feed of the Academy of Television Arts & Sciences.
3. Primetime Emmy Awards, with a URL of emmys.com: This one also seems to be the official site of the Emmy Awards, but not also the official site of the Academy of Television Arts & Sciences.

4. Primetime Emmy Award, Wikipedia, the free encyclopedia, with a URL of en.wikipedia.org: This is the Wikipedia—a free, online encyclopedia—for the awards.

5. Television Academy—Youtube, with a URL of youtube.com: This is the Emmy Awards/Television Academy's official YouTube Channel.

6. Emmy Winners 2013, with a URL of deadline.com: This is an entertainment news article with the full list of 2013 winners.

7. Emmy Winners List, with a URL of tvline.com: This is also an entertainment new article about the awards with a full list of winners.

Remind the participants that they are searching for information about the Emmy Awards. Which of these web pages they pick depends exactly on what they are looking for.

Ask the class, "if you wanted to know the history of the awards or how the statue got its design, which would you click?" (Result 1 or result 3, the official sites of the awards.)

Ask them, "if you wanted to see the full list of nominees and winners for last year, which should they click?" (Result 6 or result 7, although additional links promised on result 1, result 3, and result 4 also promise to show "nominations" or "65th Primetime Emmy Awards," which would probably have that information.)

Ask them, "if you wanted to watch video clips of the show's telecast, which link would they click?" (Result 5, the official YouTube channel for video content.)

It's apparent that depending on your question, many different websites will have the information you need. If you wanted to know about any Emmy Award controversies or ties, for example, you would want to refine your search and ask Google to retrieve results for "Emmy award controversy" or "Emmy award most nominations."

Ask the class to look again at the search results page, and notice that there are a series of links across the top of the page in gray text. The first link, "Web," appears red and with a line under it. These links refer to what kinds of results you have searched for. Click "Images" and Google will search for images of the PrimetimeEmmys. Have participants try it.

Explain that there are other ways users can use Google more expertly:

- Maps: to search for businesses or locations based on keywords and addresses/ zip codes
- Shopping: to search for products to buy
- Videos: to search for video content. *Note:* This searches video content sources beyond YouTube, although Google does own YouTube now.
- News: to search news and current events sites only
- Books: to search for print or digitized print book information

- Flights: to search for flights and flight data
- Discussions: to search comments and message boards
- Recipes: to search for recipes
- Patents: to search for patents
- And others: Google is constantly refining and improving these options

Ask the class to click Web again, to return to the list of web results. Now notice the search tools link, which is also in gray text in the same row. These search tools are what experienced Internet users call an "advanced search," because it helps limit and refine your results. Click this link and three dropdown options will appear:

- Any time: Click here to limit results to when they were published online, including preset options like "last week" as well as the capability of putting in custom date ranges
- All results: Click here to limit results from "all results" to results by reading level, by location (nearby gives local sources), and verbatim, which returns specific words.
- Location: To change the location you want to use for local search. This should be set to your geographical location as a default.

Note: Tell the class to be sure to review Google's own help pages for more comprehensive information about these dynamic search options, which change frequently. See https://support.google.com/websearch/.

Inform participants that they are going to practice another search for general information. Ask them to return to their Google search bar and type: "Rio de Janeiro" (without the quotation marks). Perform the search. This is a great time to point out that Google performs a spell check on your searches, and will interpret common misspellings and correct them. So, if anyone accidentally typed "Rio do Janeiro" or "Rio de Janiro," they will see that Google "knew" what they meant, or will return results with a message, such as, "Here are the results for Rio do Janiro, but did you mean Rio de Janeiro." If you did misspell the search, go ahead and click on "did you mean Rio de Janeiro."

Explain that again, the class is going to look at the first five search results in detail before they click anything. Remember, the title of the site is in blue (and is hyperlinked), the web address/URL is in green, and the page text preview or description is in black.

Note: The first result is an ad! Point out to the class that the first site that comes up on the list has a light yellow box around the whole result, which is one of the ways Google displays ads. In addition, draw their attention to the small text at the top of the yellow box that reads "Ad related to Rio de Janeiro."

1. Flights to Rio de Janeiro, with a URL of tam.com.br: This is a sponsored ad trying to sell you a flight to Brazil from TAM Airlines. Notice that it is surrounded by a yellow box to show that it is an advertisement.
2. Rio de Janeiro, with a URL of Wikipedia.org: This is the Wikipedia entry for the city of Rio.
3. Rio de Janeiro Tourism and Vacations, with a URL of tripadvisor.com: This is a travel review site, where users can review tourist attractions or hotels in Rio.
4. Rio de Janeiro travel guide, with a URL of wikitravel.org: This is a travel guide that is open to be edited by anyone online.
5. Rio de Janeiro City, with a URL of lonelyplanet.com: This is the Rio page from the popular travel guide publisher Lonely Planet.

Explain to the class that sometimes, Google will place news results near the top of the list if the search is for a city or person, even though they did not ask for news results. This session does not cover news results because (1) they do not appear after every search, (2) they are too dynamic to describe in print, and (3) they are clearly marked in the Google results list as "News for Rio de Janeiro."

Ask participants to review the results, and notice that these results seem all pretty credible. That is, they are from sources they can verify (such as an online encyclopedia or customer reviews or a travel guide publisher). Of course, the ad for a flight is not necessarily credible: it is an ad paid for by an airline. So as a user, if you are shopping for a flight to Brazil, you would want to search and compare many different airlines. That is one reason to question the credibility of that result.

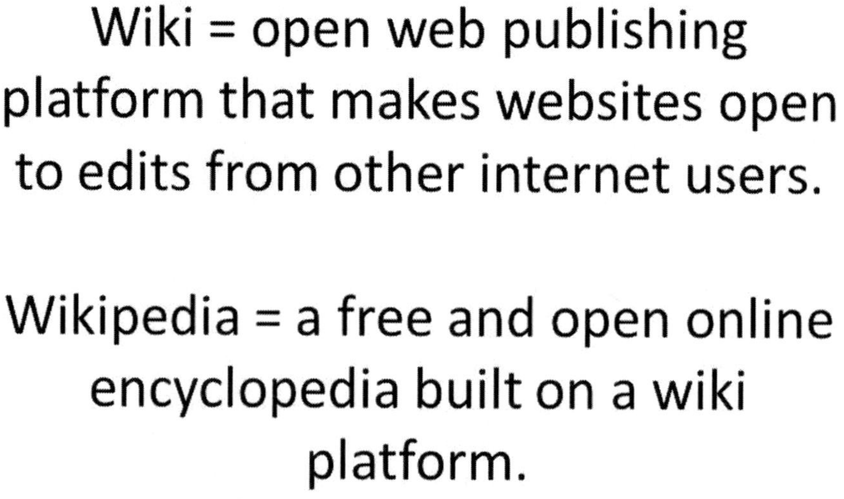

Wiki = open web publishing platform that makes websites open to edits from other internet users.

Wikipedia = a free and open online encyclopedia built on a wiki platform.

Figure 5.4   Wikipedia is just one website that uses a wiki platform.

Ask users to focus in on Result 2 and result 4. The websites Google found both have "wiki" in their name and addresses. And you have probably at least heard of Wikipedia, which is one of the sites.

Explain that Wikipedia is one of the most commonly accessed websites on the planet, and one built on a collaborative platform called a "wiki." This platform means that the website is open to be edited by anyone who signs up as a registered user. The content on Wikipedia is (not?) automatically suspect: there is an editorial process and edits are tracked and vetted. In fact, if class members are interested, suggest that you examine controversial Wikipedia entries that are edited daily or weekly by activists from opposite ideological camps. The important thing to remember is that Wikipedia is generally a fantastic tool for quick overviews of a given subject.

Have participants click on result 2 to travel to the Wikipedia entry for Rio de Janeiro.

Explain that the web browser is displaying the encyclopedia article for Rio. Ask them to glance down the left-hand side of the screen and notice that Wikipedia is available, as of 2014, in 287 language and dialect versions. The articles are not simply translations. Users will find that more common and major world languages—English, Spanish, Arabic, Chinese—have longer articles with more content, presumably because there are more speakers of those languages who are online and using the Internet.

Have the class scan the actual content on the page. Point out the boxes with data such as year founded, government structure, population, coordinates, and so on. In addition, there are several maps, as well as pictures of the city flag and seal alongside photographs of well-known landmarks in the city. Point out, too, the table of contents for the article. Explain that it is hyperlinked and makes navigating lengthy Wikipedia entries easier.

Explain to the class that ultimately, it is up to them to decide if a particular Internet site has relevant and credible information. For example, someone might be searching for information about hoaxes or extraterrestrials, and the most relevant information might not be credible at all. So depending on why they need the information, they should keep in mind that they are the ones to define relevancy. Most people don't consider Wikipedia to be credible because it is crowd-sourced, or edited by the general Internet public. One way of making sure that the information you read on Wikipedia is credible is to examine the references. Wikipedia articles have a series of hyperlinked footnotes. Some of these references are to other websites or Internet sources, and some are to print resources such as books. The Rio article has 205 references as of this writing, and four external links for further information. Try clicking through to the original source: can you verify the information claimed?

Ask users to reflect on this. Do they think they can believe this information? Is it credible? What makes it credible (or seem credible and trustworthy)?

Tell the class that now that they know the basics of doing a search for general information, they'll learn about more specialized searching. The first kind of specialized search to learn about is looking for a specific website, rather than a bunch of websites about a given topic. For example, a user might want to search for their state's unemployment compensation benefits website to register. If you just type "unemployment benefits," you will get a mix of junk results, newspaper articles about joblessness, and many, many ads inviting you apply for unemployment online (all of which are junk links!)

Explain that when they are searching, the more specific the input, the more specific the output.

When you are searching for a particular business or restaurant, for example, you should be as specific as possible. For example, ask the class to try searching "hair salon." Type "hair salon" (without the quotation marks) into Google.

Now ask them to type "hair salon pennsylvania." How are the results different? More useful? Now try "Hair salon philadelphia." How are these

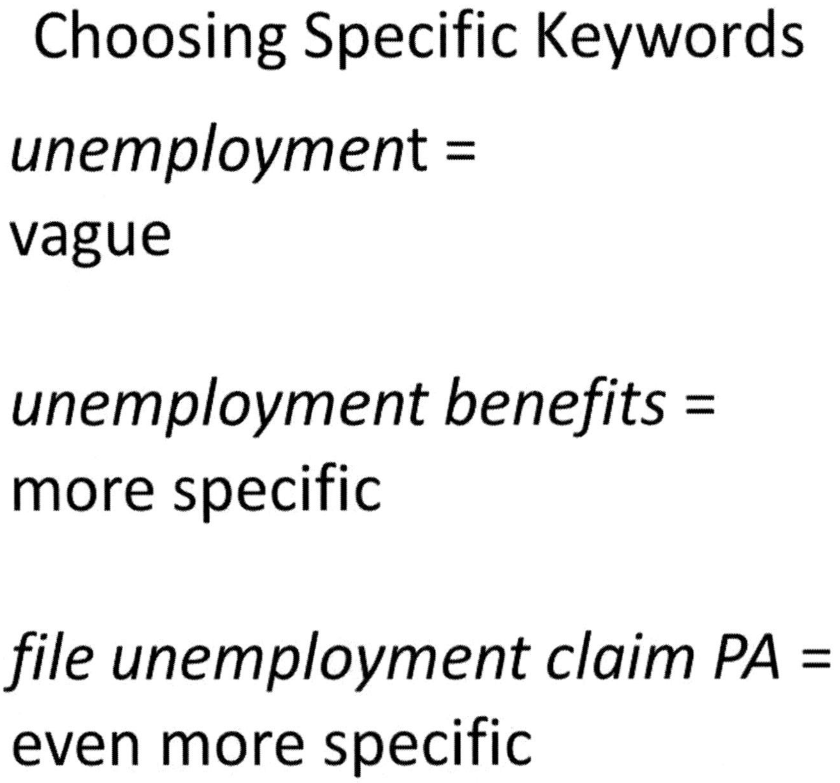

Choosing Specific Keywords

unemployment = vague

unemployment benefits = more specific

file unemployment claim PA = even more specific

Figure 5.5 The more specifically you refine search queries and input strings, the better and more relevant your results will be.

new words narrowing the results? Would this help you pick out a place to do your hair? How about searching for "Hair braiding baltimore avenue, philadelphia, pa" or "Mens hair salon baltimore avenue, philadelphia, pa." Have the participants try out some of these searches and share with the class. Ask users what are the best words or phrases they would put in to find a hair salon in a new area?

Explain to the class that the next search they are going to practice is one for jobs. If you just type "jobs" into Google, the search engine returns more than 4 billion results, including many ads. The top results are nation-wide (or even international) databases where people can list jobs. Casting such a large net means that you might find very few jobs you are interested in or qualified for. Some of these Internet-wide job sites include indeed.com, careerbuilder.com, and monster.com. These could work for some job hunters, but tell participants that it is important to remember the following tips when they are searching for jobs:

- Use keywords relating to the jobs you are looking for, and add in your city, state or zip code.
- If you want to search for local jobs at a national chain (such as Target, Home Depot, or FedEx, for example), you should travel first to the national chain's website and then look for "careers," "employment," or "jobs" links on that page. You can also try a search string such as "CVS jobs Philadelphia" or "Amtrak jobs Seattle."
- Some sites—especially big ones—will ask you to log in or even invite you to upload your resume. That might be taking valuable time away from searching for actual, live jobs. Remember that if something sounds too good to be true, on the Internet it is too good to be true. How likely is it that an employer will be scouring online resumes from complete strangers rather than waiting for applications?
- You should never have to pay any fee to apply for a job. If a particular site is asking you to pay, it is a good sign that it is a scam.
- Begin job searches by identifying large companies, organizations, universities, or institutions in your area. You can enter a search such as "largest employer 05701" or "major employers Baltimore, MD" to see a listing of large companies. Then use Google to find the websites of those companies/organizations and any open jobs they are advertising.
- Use classifieds, such as on craigslist.org. Craigslist is an Internet classifieds service where people can place ads for all sorts of goods and services, including jobs. In addition, craigslist maintains separate classifieds sites for different cities/metropolitan regions, states, or countries, so you can be sure you are finding local results. This is a great resource for restaurant (cooking and serving jobs), freelance writing work, and many other industries.

Tell the class that the final kind of search they will learn about before they have time to practice more searching is social search. Social search refers to

Hashtags (#) = way to mark a keyword or subject in a social media post.

Examples:
#BreakingBad, #Olympics, #election2016.

Figure 5.6   Hashtags mark a keyword or subject in a social media post, making them "clickable" as links to bring up all other posted tagged with that same hashtagged keyword.

searching for information posted to social networking sites, including Twitter, Facebook, and Instagram. When people post Facebook status updates or send tweets, they often include a subject term marked with a hashtag (#).

Explain that with hashtags, users can search all of Twitter, for example, for other tweets that have that same hashtag. One excellent example might be the Olympic Games. Users watching the show might "tag" their posts #Olympics or #Rio2016, which lets them connect to any other person watching the show and tweeting about it. If someone were looking for crowd-generated information and content about the Olympic Summer Games in Rio de Janeiro, the most effective way is to look at Facebook, Twitter, and Instagram posts with those same hashtags. This functionality need not be contained to one, televised event: tags like #campaign2016 or #gaymarriage are going to stay useful and relevant over a number of weeks, months, or years, and will lead users to posts tagged that way.

Ask participants to enter "hashtags.org" into the URL bar. This is a website that tracks the use of hashtags and their frequency on Twitter. You can see what hashtags (or subject keywords) are trending on Twitter, which means they are being used more frequently than other hashtags. As of this writing, for example, the site listed popular tags over all, as well as within particular categories. For example, popular hashtags in TV/entertainment included #dwts, #glee, #idol, and #xfactor.

Click on any of the #hashtags in order to see a graph of its usage, and more importantly, scroll down to see the latest tweets tagged with these subjects.

Before you continue on to more hands-on search practice, ask the class if there any questions. If not, thank them for attending this workshop about

Internet searching! Internet searching and invite them to continue practicing searches.

HANDS-ON ACTIVITIES

In each of these activities, direct users to search for information. In all cases, they can try a standard search engine, such as Google, Bing, Yahoo, or Dogpile, but there other websites to examine, as well. Instruct users to search for the keyword in a search engine, and also at the other site indicated, and then compare what they find.

A. Medical information: Use Medline, a government-funded health database. (http://www.nlm.nih.gov/medlineplus/.)

   1. Search for information about diabetes
   2. Search for information about caring for newborns
   3. Search for information about asthma
   4. Search for information about autism

B. Now try these searches in Google (or another search engine) with the term "Mayo Clinic" added to your query. You will see results from the Mayo Clinic's medical information websites. How are these different from what you found in Medline?

C. Store locations and hours: Ask class to choose a local store and search for its web page. Are its location and hours visible on the site? Now have them search the store and its address in Google Maps, and compare the information. Does Google Maps contain accurate information about the store's location and hours of operation?

D. Still using Google Maps, ask them to click "find directions" and enter in a starting location (such as their home address or the library). As they map the route using Google Maps, draw their attention to the fact that there are options for pedestrian travel, biking, driving, and using public transportation (where available). Ask the class, do they agree with this route? If they are already familiar with that store, is that the route they would take?

E. Have the class navigate to kayak.com to search for flights to buy. Kayak amalgamates searches from many different travel websites and airlines, and is fairly comprehensive. (For comparison's sake, they can try googling "flights to" and pick a city. They will see that Google is not a search engine designed to find actual flights to purchase, but is great for finding out the status of an individual flight (delayed, arrived, etc.)

NOTES

1. http://www.worldwidewebsize.com/.
2. http://gizmodo.com/30-percent-of-the-internet-is-a-copy-of-itself-1484997029.

6

Online Shopping

This chapter will help you teach beginning Internet users the basics of safe and fun online shopping. It is best done in one to two hours of instructional time, with more time for practice shopping where appropriate. During a one-hour module, you should focus just on Amazon or on eBay, and save the other online shop for a future class. Consider scheduling it before and during the holiday gift-giving frenzy of late autumn, when it will be highly relevant to many patrons.

AFTER-CLASS COMPETENCIES

After this workshop, users should be able to:

- Understand the rudiments of picking out an item for purchase and checking out of an online store
- Understand online payment options
- Identify trustworthy online retailers
- Browse and search Amazon.com
- Browse and search ebay.com
- Browse and search Google shopping
- Search for and use promotion codes or coupons

BEFORE CLASS

- Register sample accounts at the online retailers you will discuss, including Amazon.com, ebay.com, or others. You will need to be logged in as a registered user to experience the full functionality of these sites in this lesson.

KEY CONCEPTS

The following *key concepts* will be presented to learners in the training script, slides, and hands-on activities. Familiarize yourself with them and refer back to this list as needed.

Online vs. Bricks and Mortar

Bricks and mortar is the term Internet users use to refer to real, live stores that you can go inside. These are physical stores as we are used to them, with a door, a cash register, and so on. This phrase stands in contrast to online shopping, where the store and storefront are virtual or digital, and where the shopping experience happens online via a computer, tablet, or smartphone.

Browsing

Just as someone would browse in a bricks and mortar store by walking up and down the aisles, online shoppers also can go shopping without knowing particularly what they are looking for. Most online stores are organized into sections or departments, which let users click on a particular category (such as baby clothes or belts/accessories at a clothing store or tents/sleeping bags or hiking boots at an outdoor or camping supply shop). In this way, browsing online can be a lot like browsing in an actual store, and people are often shopping online with no real intention of buying things. As in real life, they are comparing different products, looking for different options (different sizes or colors, for example), or simply passing time looking. As users browse, they have the option of adding items to their shopping cart.

Logging In or Not

Most online stores can be searched and browsed without having a user account. But usually, when someone actually wants to make a purchase, the online store will invite them to create an account. So the next time a user visits that same online store, they have the option of logging in with their account username and password. Some users appreciate this as a convenience, because it means that you do not have to reenter shipping or billing information again, or perhaps because the store in question maintains a "wish list" of products that users can access without having to search for the products in question every time. Other users may feel as though they do not want the online store tracking their browsing activity and comparing it to what they have bought. In addition to privacy concerns, some online shoppers worry that they will not see all the products available at a particular store if they are logged in, because the information the store already has about them will limit their experience. This sophisticated targeting based on someone's previous browsing and buying history might lead online stores to hide or minimize some products in favor of products they think a given online shopper might be more likely to buy. Some online shoppers like this kind of targeting, because it means they will see more content and products that they are interested in. Users should experiment with these two options and see which is more comfortable and desirable.

Registering an Account or Checking Out as a Guest

When a user wants to make online purchases, they are asked to provide the online store with a lot of information. This information typically includes billing and shipping information, including names and addresses, phone numbers, and credit/debit card information. Some online stores require users to create an account that can be used every time they shop. Other online stores allow users to checkout as a guest, and enter the information without having to create a username and login that they could use again. In general, if the online shop is one a user expects to patronize again, a user account can make the experience more convenient, because it is easy to log back in to check previous charges or track shipments. Another feature you can get in most online shops by logging in is that you can add things to a shopping cart and they will stay there even if you do not buy them.

Shopping Cart

Most online stores have a virtual shopping cart or basket that users can add items to. This lets users keep an item ready for later comparison or purchasing. Nearly all online shops have links in their product information that reads "add to basket" or "add to shopping cart." Sometimes, instead of a text link, there is a small graphic of a shopping cart or basket. And depending on mobile versions of these stores and the sites displaying differently on different web browsers, the same store might make use of text links on some pages and graphical links on others. The virtual shopping cart is a key feature of any online store.

Checking Out

When users are ready to purchase the items they have selected, they will need to click a link that says "checkout" or "purchase," just as they would have to bring their purchases up to a cash register in a bricks and mortar store. There is usually a checkout link (which might say "buy" or "purchase") on every page of the store, usually near the top of the page. In addition, the shopping cart itself usually has a larger button or link near the bottom of the page for checking out. Once a user clicks "checkout" the store either (1) requires them to log in to an account, (2) allows them to checkout as a guest and brings them to the forms where they will fill out their shipping address, their billing address, pick from a variety of shipping speeds and methods, and also enter their payment information.

Shipping Address

Online stores need to send shoppers their purchases. Users therefore need to fill out a form with their shipping addresses during checkout. Users should fill this out completely, since it will be translated into a shipping label that the postal service, FedEx, or UPS will use to deliver the goods.

Billing Address

Online stores will also want a billing address, or the address that belongs to your credit/debit card account. Sometimes, this will be the same as the shipping address, and to that end, most online retailers offer a box users can click that says "same as shipping address." If it is the same address, checking this box saves a user time. Remember, though, that many users may want their goods shipped someone else as a gift, or to a work address where it is easier to receive packages.

Shipping Options

Online retailers often feature a number of different shipping options, based on the time it takes to deliver. Some have free shipping options, but the free shipping usually only cover the cheapest (and therefore often longest) delivery options. Sometimes, free shipping only kicks in if a user has spent over a certain amount, $50 or $100, for instance, or only if users have bought more than a certain number of items. Users should know that online retailers will sometimes add a default shipping charge or method that is more expensive than it needs to be. By changing the method from "3–5 days UPS ground" to "free" or "regular mail delivery," users can save themselves a lot of money!

Payment Options

The most common way to pay for something online is by using a credit or debit card. Users must provide their full credit card number, their billing zip code, and usually also the three-digit security code on the back of the card. Another common form of payment is PayPal (see below). Various online retailers have other methods, as well, including pay by electronic check/checking account or money order or by using an online-only currency such as bitcoin.

PayPal

PayPal is an online payment service owned by the online retailer eBay, but users can use PayPal to pay for a variety of online goods and services. PayPal is a third-party service, meaning that it does not belong to the online retailer in question. Some users prefer this method, especially if they are buying things from individuals or smaller online retailers and are concerned about giving out their credit card information. When using PayPal, only PayPal has the credit card or bank account information. For this reason, it is a convenient way to make transactions between individuals (i.e., paying your roommate your half of the rent money, or buying a concert ticket from an acquaintance); but it is also a very widespread practice to maintain credit card and bank account security.

Coupons and Promotions

Online retailers market aggressively, and usually have special promotions and coupons that users can use. Sometimes, previous shoppers (that is, registered users at a given online retailer) will receive emails with special offers. To redeem those special offers, there is often a code to be used at checkout. Just like at the bricks and mortar grocery store, someone has to wait until they checkout to apply their coupons. On one of the final charge, shipping and billing confirmation pages, users will see a blank field for "coupon code" or "promo code." When users enter the code, they receive the discount.

COMMON PROBLEMS AND HOW TO SOLVE THEM

The most common error is users ordering the wrong item, purchasing an item they thought they were just browsing, or being worried that their financial information is not safe when online shopping. Refer to the suggestions in the workshop plan below to explain these issues clearly, but you can also avoid these problems by instructing users not to enter any credit card or payment information until they are actually ready to buy.

WORKSHOP PLAN

Introduction: Introduce yourself to the class, and let them know they are going to learn how to use the Internet to shop. Whether participants are brand new to online shopping or already have some experience, this workshop can provide helpful information. It covers and reviews some online shopping basics that will keep users—and their credit card numbers—safe and secure.

Tell class that nearly everything can be purchased online. Clothes, books, cars, even groceries! Some people shop online because they do not have access to certain stores or products in their area. Some do it because they need to have items delivered, and some people do it just because they prefer it. There are certain downsides of online shopping: no chance to try on clothes, difficulty in judging an item's color from your computer monitor, or difficulty in ascertaining the quality of an item via your browser.

Now ask the class to share any online shopping experiences they have had. What did they buy? Where did they buy it? If some participants haven't yet shopped online but would like to, what are they interested in shopping for?

Have class members share their comments with one another.

Explain that one great of the things about online shopping is the ability to browse vast numbers of products and do comparison shopping. Once you have an item picked out, you can use its specific product numbers or label name in a search engine and find (1) more products like it for sale by other vendors and (2) reviews of the product. This workshop introduces participants to two major online retailers, Amazon and eBay. Explain that most online shops function similarly, so what users learn about Amazon and eBay will help them browse and shop at many online retailers.

Show/tell users: Type www.amazon.com in your browser's uniform resource locator (URL) window and hit enter. Your browser will travel to Amazon.com.

When you get to the site, explain that this is the Amazon storefront. That word—storefront—is important. Remember, an online shop's web page should be the virtual version of an in-person trip to a store or mall. So, the front of the online store—just as in a brick and mortar store—is designed by marketers to get potential customers to shop. Have the class take a few moments to examine the Amazon storefront, and note some of the features they see. For example, there are deals and sales advertised along the right-hand side.

Explain that Amazon, like most online stores, is organized into departments. On the top left-hand side of the page, there is a link to "shop by department." This is subject to change based on what Amazon is currently promoting and whether or not their site navigation has changed, but expect to see categories such as these:

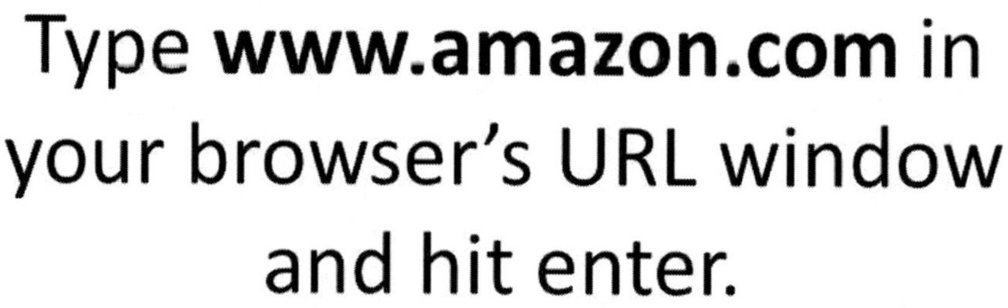

Type **www.amazon.com** in your browser's URL window and hit enter.

Figure 6.1   Use screenshots such as this one if you do not have access to a live desktop while you are teaching.

Sample Amazon Departments

Unlimited Instant Videos
MP3s & Cloud Player
Amazon Cloud Drive
Kindle E-readers
Kindle Fire Tablets
Appstore for Android
Digital Games & Software
Books & Audible
Movies, Music & Games
Electronics & Computers
Home, Garden & Tools
Beauty, Health & Grocery
Toys, Kids & Baby
Clothing, Shoes & Jewelry
Sports & Outdoors
Automotive & Industrial

Figure 6.2   Here are categories Amazon features in the category drop-down menu.

Tell users that it is important to remember that there is one key way that this store differs from a store they could actually visit at the mall. That difference is that Amazon also sells digital and downloadable products: videos you can watch on your computer, smartphone or tablet, eBooks that you can read on your Kindle or tablet, or songs to download to play on your smartphone, computer, or MP3 player. It's good to mention this at this point and caution the students to be sure to read carefully the product descriptions. If they are looking to buy a print book or an actual, physical CD of music that they can put into a CD player, look for those specifications in the production description. It is all too easy to accidentally buy a digital version of something! This is mostly a problem for books, music, and movies/television, but it is a good reminder that even something such as pots and pans or camping supplies might be very different than you expect when it is posted online. Read carefully!

Remind the class that most websites offer increased functionality and options to users who have made an account and who have logged in to the site in question. Shopping sites are no different, and often invite a user (or require a user) to log in, especially once they try to pay for something. Logging in offers increased convenience as a shopper: when a user logs in, the site can store shipping and billing addresses and/or payment preferences. In addition, users can check on shipping and delivery or track a package when they log in to their accounts, or print an additional receipt from a past purchase.

Explain to the class that they are using public computers that other people have access to. If they do log in to your account from a public computer, they should *not* agree to have the browser save their login information, including username or password. While having the browser to remember and store this information is a convenience on a personal device—a personal computer or smartphone—it is a potential risk on a public computer. Remember that online shoppers usually pay with credit cards, and users want to keep your credit card information as private as possible.

Tell the class that if they already have Amazon accounts and want to log in, go ahead. There is a useful feature to use when logged in called the "wish list." This works a lot like a gift registry by letting you add any product to a "wish" list of purchases that you can revisit later or share with friends and family. If you are logged in, you can find it by hovering over "your account" at the upper right of the Amazon page and then clicking "your wish list."

Note: If you are not logged in, the link in the header says "your" account or wish list. When you are logged in, it uses your name, that is, "Joel's" account or wish list.

Tell users that they can click on any of the products advertised on the front page, or they can browse a department. They can also search using the search box at the top of the screen. Near the left side of the box is an additional drop-down menu that allows users to search for a given product in just one department.

Amazon Account Navigation

Hello, Joel   Try   1   Wish
Your Account ▾   **Prime ▾**   ▾•• **Cart ▾**   **List ▾**

Click to:
1. access your account settings,
2. see what is in the shopping cart
3. display your wish list.

Figure 6.3   A close up of the account navigation, shopping cart, and wish list links on Amazon.com.

Announce to the class that the group is going to search for some of the same products together, and learn about what you find. Ask them to type "vacuum" into the search box and click "Go."

Explain that the search results page can be overwhelming. Have students take a couple moments to look over the page. Down the left-hand side of the page are all results, listed by department, as well as subcategories for different kinds of vacuums. From this side menu, you could narrow to see all the handheld vacuums or all the canister vacuums, in addition to products in categories you may not have expected, including toys and games (for toy vacuums) and special vacuums for cars in the automotive department.

Draw the class's attention to the fact that below the department links, there are also other ways of refining a search. As of this writing, "vacuum" returned more than 225,000 Amazon results. That is probably too many products to browse! So, you can see further refinement options, including:

Products eligible for free shipping

Product features (such as bagless, HEPA filtration, corded, etc.)

Brands (from Dyson to Oreck and many others)

Color

Condition (new or used)

Average customer review (from 1 to 5 stars)

Explain to the class that they can choose to refine their vacuum search based on any of these criteria. Try out a few by selecting:

HEPA filtration

Hoover

New

Four stars and up

As of this writing, narrowing the search based on those four criteria resulted in four vacuum cleaners to compare. And at the top of the screen, all of the criteria selected appear, and narrow my search in a navigation string that shows which department we are shopping in as well as what characteristics we are looking for.

Explain that each of these characteristics is also a link. So if users want to widen their search for a vacuum again, they could click on just one. Ask participants to practice, by clicking on HEPA filtration.

Note that you are now back up to 687 vacuums to browse, all of which offer HEPA filtration. Amazon offers additional ways to view these 687 products to make them easier to review. The first options are located just to the right of where it displays the number of results, in this search 687. There are two links: one for "detail" and one for "image."

The top of your Amazon page should show:

Home & Kitchen › Vacuums & Floor Care › Vacuums › HEPA Filtration › Hoover › New › 4 Stars & Up › "vacuum"

Figure 6.4   Amazon features "bread crumb" navigation that helps users trace their path through the site as Hansel and Gretel tried to trace theirs. Each > above shows a transition to a different subset of limited search results.

Two ways of browsing Amazon

Detail = shows product image, name, price, preview of reviews/rankings.

Image= shows product image, name and price only. This is a more visual and less text-heavy way to browse on Amazon.

Figure 6.5   Amazon offers two different ways of browsing products, detail, and image.

Explain that in addition to browsing just images or details, users can also sort these results. Have participants look for the drop-down menu toward the top right of the page that says "sort by." Mention that they can ask Amazon to list the vacuum cleaners according to a variety of attributes to make it easier for them to shop.

Tell the class that the ways they can view the products are by relevance, by new and popular, by price: low to high, by price: high to low, and by average customer review.

Explain that the group will now look at one product in detail. *Note:* Users can click on any available vacuum cleaner, or search for the specific one that will be discussed.

Show the class how to access the product page discussed here, by entering "Oreck Commercial 2100RHS 8 Pound Commercial Upright Vacuum, Blue" into the Amazon search field at the top of the page and clicking go. (*Note:* Any vacuum will work!)

Explain that you are now on a product page. Point out the same frame of links that appear around the top of the page (your account, your cart, etc.) as well as other links that have changed now that we are in a specific product category.

Ways to sort Amazon results

Relevance: ranks products based on your inputs, in this case "vacuum" and HEPA filtration

New and Popular: ranks new and best-selling products higher

Price: low to high: ranks the cheapest item first and most expensive last

Price: high to low: ranks the most expensive item first and the least expensive item last

Average Customer Review: ranks the products with the highest number of stars first

Figure 6.6   When you have a lot of results to browse through, sort them based on a variety of helpful criteria, including price, date, popularity, and so on.

Draw participants' attention to the product's full name and model number, as in a headline. Underneath is the hyperlinked name of the company offering the product, in this case Oreck Commercial. Then, they will see the list price crossed out, the price in large, red text, and underneath that the difference or "savings" price. Remind the class that, just as in any store, these "savings" are manufactured to increase sales and make it seem like you are getting a good deal. While there may be times when prices are radically reduced for certain items, users can expect that Amazon will always have a "list price" that is higher than the "actual price." It bears repeating that this is mostly about sales.

Point out the photograph of the product in the upper left of the screen. Explain that sometimes, as is this case with this vacuum cleaner, there are also customer images. Mouse over the small thumbnail images underneath the large product image and they will magnify. Seeing customer images is a great way to see what the product actually looks like!

Note that there is a lot more information to unpack on this page! Under the price information, users can see whether or not the item is in stock, and they can find other shipping information. This product says, for example, "Ships from and sold by Amazon.com in easy-to-open packing. Gift wrap available." This information is important because Amazon sells its own stock, along with acting as a marketplace for many different online stores and sellers to sell their stock.

In sum, Amazon is a store that sells its own products. Amazon is also an online marketplace that allows other stores to sell their products.

Instruct the class that shortly they will examine the differences between buying an item from Amazon itself and buying an item through Amazon, from another retailer. For a quick preview, note that there are "more buying choices" for this item, including used vacuums for sale and new ones for sale from different stores. This information is located just below the product information the class was just looking at; and is also noticeable right under the yellow shopping cart image and "Add to cart" button. Note that all of this information that the class has discussed appears at the top of the page, and that there is a thin horizontal gray line that separates it from what is below.

Explain to participants that if they read farther down the page, they can see "specifications for this item." Here are more specifics, such as size, color specifications, weight, and so on. Next, draw their attention to the row of product advertisements under the banner headline that reads "customers who bought this item also bought." Mention that, of course, this is a way Amazon is trying to get you to browse and hopefully buy more items that are related to the main product you are browsing. There are big gray buttons with arrows on them on their side of this banner/ribbon. Users can click them to advance through five screens of related products.

Tell the class to keep scrolling down the page to see product features, product details, a narrative product description, and then a series of customer reviews. Depending on the product in question, the amount of available information varies. When products have many customer reviews, users can see the ones voted (by other shoppers) as most helpful on the left-hand part of the screen and the most recent reviews on the right-hand side.

Note that users will also see Amazon advertising many related and unrelated products throughout this page, and also shows items they have recently viewed, as well as items that were purchased by other customers who looked at this item. These product links and advertisements are all automatically generated by the user's behavior on the site.

Explain that big data refers to the information a company like Amazon knows about them and other customers just from their browsing for a few minutes. They—and other Internet companies, services, and web pages—collect and store massive amounts of information every second about every user. They know everything from what items they looked it before they bought to how long they stayed on that page, and so on. The "big" part of the term refers both to the amount of information collected, as well as what that information can tell about a user. When all of this information from Amazon is compiled and cross referenced with other sets of "big data," say from Facebook or Twitter, there is a lot of information about shoppers! For this reason, some of the class might prefer not to shop online at all. Explain that this information is covered at length not to scare anyone away from using Internet technology, but rather to illuminate the murky landscape and to remind them that their Internet behavior is being watched, and has consequences. It is never truly anonymous or private, and it is in fact used by companies to more effectively sell users things.

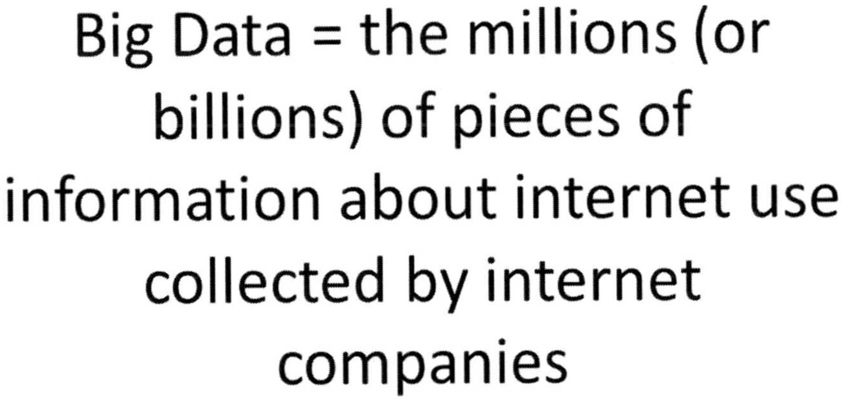

Big Data = the millions (or billions) of pieces of information about internet use collected by internet companies

Figure 6.7   Offer key terms defined in clear type and without too much verbiage. Here, users see a simplified definition of big data that is relevant to their experience levels.

Explain that you are now going to walk the class through the process of buying this vacuum cleaner. Note if you were actually shopping, you would probably want to browse more options, compare more customer or other reviews, and maybe even look for a lower price on another site. But for now, the class will use this product to practice buying it. So participants have their vacuum cleaners picked out and are ready to put them in their shopping carts.

Show the class how to click "Add to cart," which is a yellow button with a picture of a shopping cart on it.

Explain that Amazon also has a feature, for registered users, to buy something with "1-click." When users are logged in, they can purchase an item immediately (without "checking out" by clicking "buy with 1-click." This feature is best reserved for more advanced Internet shoppers.

Tell the class that when they have added the vacuum cleaner to their carts, the page will resolve to a new page that shows, in green text, that you have "1 item added to cart."

At this point, users can also designate whether the item is a gift. If it is a gift, Amazon will "Hide the item in an Amazon shipping box or the contents may be visible when delivered" and "Include a packing slip so the recipient knows who it's from." There are also gift-wrapping options.

Announce that users now have this vacuum in their shopping carts. Note that the web page offers two options with buttons near the right-hand side of the screen. These buttons are "edit your cart" and "proceed to checkout." Explain that clicking "edit your cart" applies if they to make changes—to delete the vacuum, or to buy two of them, for instance. Tell them that clicking "proceed to checkout" completes their purchases.

Show the class how to click "proceed to checkout."

Note that at this time, users will have to log in with an Amazon account to continue.

Explain that if they have already used Amazon before, they will see all of the following information on the next screen, the review your order screen:

- Shipping address
- Billing address
- Payment method
- Order summary that includes item(s) cost, shipping and handling, pretax total, estimated tax to be collected, and order total cost
- Estimated delivery options and prices for each option
- A "place your order" button that must be clicked to actually make the purchase

Tell participants that if they want to change any of this information—for example, to update an expired credit card—they should click the small blue link next to the options above that reads "change." For shipping speed and prices, users can click the different radio buttons to see different price and time options. Amazon helpfully shows customers, in green text, how these shipping options match up to the calendar. You should see, for example, next to one-day shipping it says "get it tomorrow," with tomorrow's date.

Explain that those who do not have Amazon accounts will be asked to enter all of this information into form blanks. This process is similar to filling out the blanks to sign up for an email account.

Note: Refer to the following *key concepts* described earlier in this chapter for more information about "shipping address," "billing address," "shipping options," and "payment options."

Now announce: Congratulations! You just bought a vacuum. Well, you have not, actually, but this is exactly how you would have.

Instruct the class that you are now going to look briefly at another online store, eBay. Ebay.com is a very large Internet retailer, but it operates differently from Amazon. It is structured as an auction site, where individuals can put items up for sale or bid. Then, other buyers from around the world can search those listings, make bids on items and buy them.

Navigate to ebay.com.

Ask the class to take a few moments to look at this homepage. It is structured much like Amazon.com, in that there are many different navigation options along the top of the page. These include, at the very top of the page, the invitation to sign in to an existing account or to register a new account, along with a link to "daily deals," a "sell" link for users interested in putting up items for sale, "customer support" for help, and then, toward the right-hand side of the window, "my eBay," a bell-shaped pictogram for notifications and a shopping cart link.

Remind participants that just as on Amazon.com, they can browse without being logged in. But the most full customer experience results from being logged in, and the "my eBay" and Notifications links they just saw would be full of personalized information.

Explain that the next set of navigation links include a "shop by category" drop-down and a search box. Users can search for an item across all categories or specify a category in which to search by selecting the specific category from the right-hand drop-down menu. Note that there are two category drop-down menus, one to the left of the search box and one to the right. Use the one on the left to browse by category, and the one on the left to limit a search by category.

Show users the eBay categories, and explain that they include collectibles and art, electronics, entertainment, fashion, home and garden, and motors.

Ask the class to practice searching for an item so they can compare those results to Amazon results.

Tell participants to type "vacuum cleaner" into the search field, not limiting the category by using the drop-down to the right. Explain that while they could limit to "home & garden," and might want to, they should get an overview first.

Instruct class to click "search" and then look at the results. It should look similar to Amazon in that product names, photographs, and prices appear. But there are many other pieces of information on this page that users would not find on Amazon.

Draw the class's attention to the top of the white box that frames all the results. Remind them that web designers use things like colored or shaded boxes and lines to help users navigate pages. Along the top of this white box framing the results, they should see that there are three buttons:

All listings: This option is shaded and in black text, showing that it is selected. This option shows all results, more than 47,000 for this case.

Auction: This option appears in blue text, showing that it is not selected. It will display all the item listings that are auctions.

Buy it now: This option is also in blue, showing that it is not selected. It will display all the item listings that are available to be purchased without bidding.

Explain that although eBay is an auction site, some people selling items on this online store also offer some of those items for straight sale without bidding. Any of those "buy it now" items can be purchased immediately.

Show the class how to click on "auction," so they can see what a live eBay auction looks like. Notice that all of these new results (now down from 48,000 and some change to a little over 2,000 items) are auctions. The results page still shows a photograph of the object and the current bidding price. Note that there is also an auction timer, in orange text, showing how long until the auction is over. The ones at the top of the list are the auctions closing soonest, so they the time left on those auctions is usually in the seconds or minutes. And underneath the price, users can also see how many bids have been made.

Click on the sort drop-down menu to show the class the many ways they can sort eBay search results. These include options by time (most time left to bid/least time left to bid), distance to/from a given zip code, price (low to high) and price of item with shipping added in (low to high), and number of bids (most first or least first). Tell users to experiment with these options, to see what is available.

Click on an open auction, and tell class that you will now examine an auction page.

Show them the open auction, asking them to notice the primary image of the object, as well as more images located underneath it. Mouse over those smaller images to magnify them. Point out the right-hand side of the page, where they will see more product information.

Explain that the information they can see here is all about one individual item for sale. Point out:

- Item headline/description.
- Item condition: Is it new? Used? Refurbished?
- Time left to bid: How much longer the auction will be open.
- Starting bid: The number of bids already placed and an empty text box in which you could place a new bid, next to a blue button that reads "place bid."
- Add to watch list: Adds this item to your personalized eBay watch list to get updates as others bid.
- Add to collection: Adds item to a wish list/personalized collection of eBay items; does not mean that you are going to buy it.
- Shipping: Shows the item's location and estimated cost of standard shipping.
- Delivery estimate: A date when it could be delivered.
- Payment options: eBay accepts PayPal for all purchases, but individual sellers may also accept other options, such as "bill me later." Note that "bill me later" is like applying for a store credit card and you will have to wait for credit check/approval before you can pay with this option.
- Returns options: eBay does not allow buyers to return all items. This information will inform you about terms and options for returning any unwanted merchandise.
- Guarantee: eBay does guarantee that you will get the item you ordered or your money back. Note that this does not take into account the situation where you received an item but that it was not what you wanted for some reason. This guarantee protects you from outright scammers who would sell you a nonexistent item.

Ask participants to scroll to the bottom to see larger photographs and more product description. Remind them that this is their only opportunity to see the object/item in question from different angles or in different views, and to read what the seller has posted about it. Note, too, that like Amazon, there are many sponsored links advertising other products, showing you what other people who looked at this item also shopped for, and what else shoppers are watching int. Although these additional products are designed to make you click and buy, they can also just browse them.

Tell users to look to the right of the "place bid" button and notice the white box with the heading "seller information." Note that the seller's name is a blue hyperlink. Click on it to go to their user page. This page offers a wealth of information that can help users decide if this is a seller they want to purchase something from. Notice that under their name, there is a percentage listed of how much positive feedback they have received from other buyers. Users can also see links for (1) what other items they have for sale, (2) visiting their storefront, and (3) contacting them.

Have participants assume they are on the lookout for vintage vacuums, and they have determined that this eBay seller is a merchant to keep an eye on so they can be alerted whenever they post a new vintage vacuum for sale. Click "follow," which is a green button with a plus sign on it to follow this seller. This makes is easier to find them the next time you come back and log in to eBay.

Explain that from here on out, they could place bids on items or buy something right away. Remind them that eBay has been around for almost a decade, and in that time, many people all over the world have become professional (or at least full-time) eBay buys and sellers. As a result, novice users should take their time to investigate the site and particular sales before they spend any money. In addition, it is recommended that users new to eBay look at several eBay help pages, including:

Ebay getting started guide (http://pages.ebay.com/help/account/gettingstarted .html) for a general overview of registering the account (Google keywords: ebay help getting started)

How Do I Buy an Item on eBay? (http://pages.ebay.com/help/buy/questions/ buy-item.html) for an overview of the purchasing and paying systems (Google keywords: ebay how do i buy an item)

Tips and Tricks for eBay Buying and Selling (http://www.ebay.com/gds/Tips-and-Tricks-for-eBay-Selling-and-Buying-/10000000001367075/g.html) for a guide written by an eBay user with helpful, expert tips for beginners (Google keywords: Tips and Tricks for eBay Selling and Buying)

31 Key Tricks and Tips About Ebay (http://www.ebay.com/gds/31-KEY-TRICKS-AND-TIPS-ABOUT-EBAY-/10000000004021629/g.html) for another user-generated guide with expert tips. (Google keywords: 31 key tricks tips ebay)

HANDS-ON ACTIVITIES

A. Tell users to look for an item of interest (or a vacuum cleaner) on Craigslist .org. Direct them to navigate to craigslist.org, verify their city/state local link and then to start searching for vacuums. (*Note:* As described earlier, craigslist.org is a place for classified ads. This is "online shopping" in a way, but involves real-life, in-person payment and pick-up/delivery, just as if you were buying someone's used sofa off the grocery store bulletin board).

B. Now ask users to search for the same product (any product of their choice) on Amazon.com and by using Google search—>shopping. Remind them that this is a good time to used tabbed browsing, so they can switch back and forth between the various sites with ease. Ask them the following questions: Are they finding the same products? Are they the same prices? Same shipping price? What about the various online retailers they are visiting in their search: Do some seem better or more reliable than others? What are the differences that make them feel secure or not in this online shopping?

C. Coupons and promo codes. Instruct users to Google search "Amazon promo codes" and examine the results together. What kinds of coupons and promotions are being offered? How easy would it be to find them for another online retailer? Using some of the additional retailers they found in activity 2 mentioned earlier, search for more promotion codes or coupons (for example "target promo code," "home depot online coupon," "overstock.com coupon code," and "threadless tshirts promo code" as Google search strings).

D. Direct users to etsy.com. Tell them that this is an online shop where individuals put items up for sale that are often homemade, so shopping here is similar to shopping at a garage sale, flea market, or arts and crafts sale. Etsy, like Amazon or eBay, is also organized by categories. Individual sellers on Etsy have storefronts, much like individuals on eBay. Encourage them to search for (a) one item that is used or vintage, and (b) one item that is homemade. What do they notice that is the same or different, shopping on Etsy compared to their other online shopping experiences? What about the breadth of products on sale? Why might they use this retailer, that is, purchase from individuals via a website, rather than using an online mega-retailer, such as Target.com or Amazon.com? What are some of the advantages or disadvantages?

E. Encourage any willing users to register an Amazon.com account, and have them make a wish list. They should search for 5–10 products they would really like to buy or receive and make a wish list of them.

F. Direct users to http://www.amazon.com/gp/feature.html?docId=1001250201 (Google search string "funny amazon reviews"). Tell them that there is an online culture around Amazon reviews, and that some users have written sarcastic and ironic reviews of products on purpose. Have them read the reviews for BIC Cristal for Her Ball Pen, a BIC pen marketed specifically for women. What do they think of those reviews? Are there any products they would like to write a review for? Encourage any users with an Amazon.com to write an actual product review for a product or item they may already have.

7

Dating Online

This chapter introduces learners to the basics of online dating, including profiles, how to find a dating or personals site, and some safety tips.

AFTER-CLASS COMPETENCIES

After this workshop, users should be able to:

- Identify a dating website appropriate for them
- Establish an online dating profile
- Understand how they are sharing personal information on their dating profile

KEY CONCEPTS

The following *key concepts* are presented to learners in the training script, slides, and hands-on activities. Familiarize yourself with them and refer back to this list as needed.

Kinds of Websites

There are many different kinds of websites for dating and meeting people on and offline. Sometimes, they are very specific services designed to match people with similar religious beliefs (such as ChristianMingle.com or Jdate, for Jewish singles), or with similar cultural backgrounds (Blackplanet.com for African Americans or Migente.com for Latinos). There are also LGBTQ (lesbian, gay, bisexual, transgendered, and queer) dating sites. Many additional sites, services, and apps are primarily designed to connect people for sexual encounters via personal ads, so it is important that users understand the breadth and depth of different ways to meet someone online.

Profile

The cornerstone of online dating at many sites is to create a profile. This functions somewhat (and looks) like a social networking profile users may be familiar with from Facebook, but Internet daters must take care and preserve more privacy in a dating profile. Users should think twice before sharing personal information such as address, phone number, or even email in a dating profile, even less often than they appear on other social networking services. In addition, listing a place of employment, last name, or sharing other identifying information that would make it easy for others to find them in the real world without an explicit invitation is discouraged. But at the same time, dating profiles do need some specific and personal information: hobbies and interests, likes and dislikes, what kind of date you are looking for, as well as photographs.

Searching Profiles

Most Internet dating sites offer the ability to search through profiles. Users can usually set limits using search filters, to search for other dating profiles that fit a certain criteria. Every site has slightly different criteria, but in general, most have the following capabilities: limit results by age, by gender, by same-, bi-, or heterosexual interest, and by zip code or distance from a certain zip code. In addition, many allow users to sort and limit the profiles they see by weight/height, by race, by religious beliefs if any, and so on. Some sites might automatically suggest profiles to look at based on a user's demographic information in a profile as well as these kinds of search.

Private Messages

Because many online daters are rightly reluctant to share too much personal information too quickly, most dating websites have a private message feature for users to exchange written messages. These are like emails, except that they are sent via a user's email account. Users can assume that these messages are reasonably private, but should remember that anyone gaining access to their profile can also read them. Some online daters exchange several messages via this method from inside their profiles before they trade phone numbers or email addresses for arranging an in-person meeting.

Sharing Photos

The best online dating profiles have at least one accurate photograph of the user. Some services stipulate that users need to have a clear face picture, while others allow users to upload any photo file (an avatar, an illustration, etc.) to be the profile photo. Most services have strict rules about nudity or explicitly sexual situations, and do not allow anything "not safe for work" as the public profile. Most dating sites allow users to mark some photographs as public and some as private, meaning that you can invite others to see your private ones on a case-by-case basis. Depending on the dating site in question and the user, however, people often do include intimate photos among their private photos. Users should be made aware of the risks this opens up that their photos (even the private ones) could be copied and shared without their permission.

Privacy and Linking Accounts

Remember that, although users need to use an email account to sign up for a dating service, they do not need to make their email address or other social media (Twitter, Facebook, or Instagram) profile viewable via their dating profile. Dating sites ask users to do this as a default, and may even employ crafty web design that either tricks a user into adding their other profiles or makes it hard or confusing to opt out. Internet daters, especially inexperienced ones, should not rush to expose more information about themselves in this other public forum. Experienced users might not see the harm in giving out their email address via a dating profile, but they still need to exercise caution.

Smartphone Apps for Dating/Socializing

While smartphone apps use the Internet to exchange data and information between the user and others, they do not work in a browser-based environment on computers. But users should be aware of them, particularly as more and more folks are using smartphones that allow them Internet connectivity outside the library. There are apps that offer unique dating/social functions, including ones that use your phone's GPS to help connect you with other folks who might be nearby. Tinder is one such app that shows you the Facebook profiles of people within certain, set geographical limits. For gay men, the apps Scruff, Growlr, and Grindr function similarly, although rather than using Facebook profiles, they offer their own personals profile.

WORKSHOP PLAN

Introduce yourself and tell users that this workshop is about online dating and will help them understand how dating websites work, give them information about creating a profile or personal ad, and identify potential dating websites to use.

Note: Because of the somewhat sensitive nature of online dating, it is not a good idea to walk users through reviewing or creating profiles. The potential for uncomfortable interactions with people's sexual or personal

Pick a dating site that's right for you!

Blackplanet.com, Migente.com, Outpersonals.com, OK Cupid, Jdate.com, ChristianMingle.com...

which ones appeal to your life and community?

Figure 7.1 When dealing with sensitive topics such as sex or dating, be as direct as possible. Keep reminding participants that they are in charge and that they are the ones who decide if a site is relevant to them.

lives is too high for library workers to engage this subject matter intimately. However, the following slides and information will help users understand Internet dating and various ways to share, and you can give them time and space to pursue their own dating profiles at the end of the workshop. Offer as much advice as you are comfortable with, but do not be afraid to remind your participants about what kinds of personal information you *do not* want to see on library computers.

Explain to the class that there are a lot of different kinds of dating websites. There are large, commercial ones that cost money to use. These include Eharmony.com, which matches up users with potential dates based on a long questionnaire. Most dating sites give free (or ad-supported) access to at least some parts of their services.

Stress that there are many different kinds of sites! Some of the large ones, such as OK Cupid, have broad user bases that include lots of people of different religions, ethnic or linguistic backgrounds, sexualities, among others. Others, such a Jdate, will naturally be more limited to a particular subgroup (in this case, Jewish people).

Explain that the cornerstone of every online dating and social media service is a profile. This is personal information displayed for the Internet community. Be sure users know that everything they post to their profiles could potentially be seen by their bosses, their parents, their significant others, their children, their coworkers, and so on. Information published to the Internet never really goes away, even if you attempt to delete it. Tell participants to keep this in mind and not overshare!

Tell users that profiles usually include a screen name, which is also the username a user would use to log in to a particular site. Profiles also usually include a picture or pictures, basic information such as age, location (by zip code or city), race/ethnicity, gender, and so on. Additionally, there may be a place in a profile for weight, height, occupation, hair color, eye color, interests, hobbies, and so on. This information is not all required.

Instruct the class that once they have filled out an online profile, they can then use the dating site's search functionality to search and view the profiles of others. The exact functionalities vary by site, but in general, users are usually able to limit results by age, by gender, by same-, bi-, or heterosexual interest, and by zip code or distance from a certain zip code. In addition, many allow users to sort and limit the profiles they see by weight/height, by race, by religious beliefs if any, and so on.

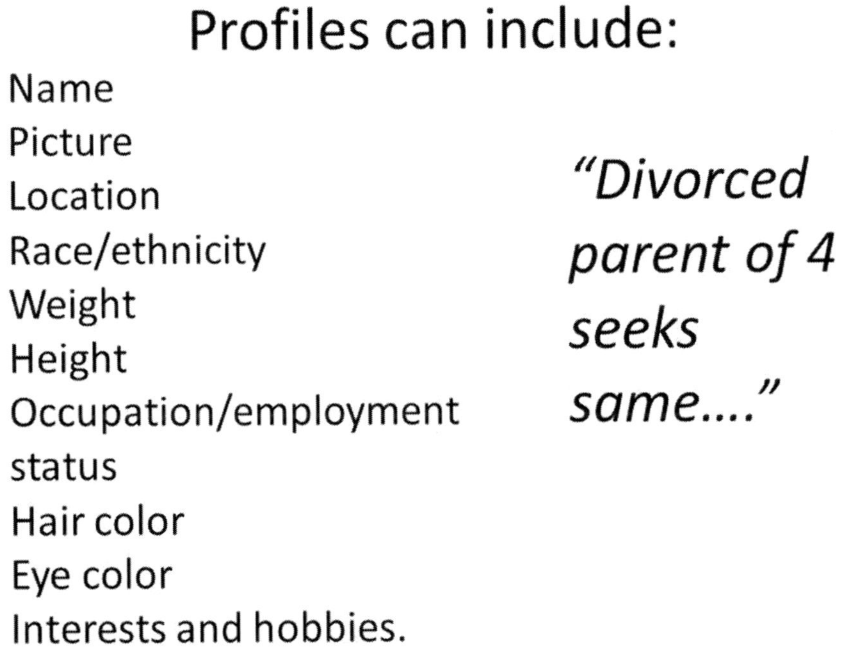

Profiles can include:

Name
Picture
Location
Race/ethnicity
Weight
Height
Occupation/employment
status
Hair color
Eye color
Interests and hobbies.

"Divorced parent of 4 seeks same...."

Figure 7.2 Dating profiles show a lot of basic but personal information. Remind participants that they are not required to disclose any information about themselves just because a web page suggests they do!

Explain that most dating sites use a personal messaging system, which functions like email, but which allow users to send text and pictures without disclosing their email addresses. These are called private messages. Remember, though, although they are "private," and users have to log in to access them, anything they send via these private messages are the property of the dating service/website and may be inadvertently exposed.

Tell the class that people dating online usually share photographs of themselves. Most services have strict rules about nudity or explicitly sexual situations, and do not allow anything "not safe for work" as the public profile. Most dating sites allow users to mark some photographs as public and some as private, meaning that they can invite others to see their private ones on a case-by-case basis. Depending on the dating site in question and the user, however, people often do include intimate photos among their private ones.

HANDS-ON ACTIVITIES

Encourage workshop participants to work independently on their profiles, or to practice searching personal ads of one of the sites mentioned earlier.

8

Community: Lives Online

This chapter will help you show beginning Internet users some of the social options available to people online, including sharing music, video, or pictures. It is best done in a one- to two-hour block of time.

AFTER-CLASS COMPETENCIES

After this workshop, users should be able to:

- Understand the Digital Millennium Copyright Act (DMCA) and the way it limits sharing music or video files
- Search and find message boards
- Decode message board slang
- Create and share invitations to events on Facebook or Eventbrite

KEY CONCEPTS

Sharing Online

A key feature of online communities is sharing information: personal information or writing, photographs, opinions, and links to things like news stories, music videos, or other short online videos. Users should be made to understand that when they share anything online, companies get access to that data. A company like Facebook can run sophisticated analyses of who posted which links, who clicked on and read which links, and a lot of other data. This information is usually only available to employees of the company, and the specific ways they intend to use the data are spelled out in the user agreement an Internet user agrees to when they are first signing up. Remind users that sometimes sharing web links on a social media or Internet profile can show other people that user's Internet activity in a way they did not intend.

Sharing Music

Users may be interested in sharing music. There are many ways to do this. They can email or attach music files such as MP3 files to posts on social media. This method works best if users own the rights to the music file in question. If not, another common way to share music is by posting a link from some streaming music or video file (such as a music video on YouTube, for example) to someone's social media feed. In addition, there are special social media websites and services that are designed just to connect users based on music. The most popular of these is called Spotify, and lets users listen to music for free and created shared playlists to send to others. Spotify is useful for beginning users because it is legal, and users do not need to worry about unintentionally violating the DMCA.

Digital Millennium Copyright Act (DMCA) and Digital Rights Management (DRM)

Beginning Internet users often assume that everything is available online, and that everything is available for free online. While there are many sites where users can illegally access (via download) almost any content they desire, from Hollywood blockbuster movies to eBooks and whole albums, most of the legal ways of accessing music and video content cost money. They cost in part because the DMCA makes it necessary to pay the copyright holders for accessed materials. This often means that when a user buys a song from iTunes or the Google Play stores, or an eBook from Amazon, the files have a built-in DRM, which locks down the file and makes it hard or impossible to copy, modify, or share more widely. DMCA and DRM are very controversial topics, with copyright holders and production companies trying to protect profits on the one hand, and a somewhat radical philosophy of open and free access to all information, all the time on the other. Most Internet users will find themselves in the middle of these two camps, so it is necessary to educate them about the legality of sharing music and videos online. It is also worthwhile to introduce the other side of the argument, for free and open access.

Creative Commons Licenses

In response to closed copyright, a movement to offer licensed content that users can download for free, remix, and adulterate, as well as share more widely themselves has sprung up: creative commons. This is a kind of copyright license that lets content creators stipulate exactly what users can do with their content (text, photographs, music, or video) for free and without asking permission. These licenses provide a great way to learn about fair use and other copyright issues. Their mission is to build an infrastructure of content and rules for that content in order to maximize users' potential to creatively engage and share with other artistic and creative endeavors. Users making and posting their own web content should investigate realizing it under a creative commons license. The website has an easy to use tool that helps users select a license. Users must decide, for example, if they will let others modify their work in anyway, and if they will allow any commercial use of their work. It also stipulates very clearly how the work should be attributed to the creator to help make sure others are not passing off someone else's work as their own.

Comments and Message Boards

Another way people share ideas and information online is via comments and message boards. Most blogs offer commenting facility, and so do many news websites and other services. Thousands—or even millions at this point—of web services have also integrated Facebook commenting into their sites, so users can actually use their Facebook accounts to comment on a given Internet web link or news story. Some blogs and sites allow users to post a comment anonymously, although being able to maintain anonymity is harder and harder as more sites require a username/login to post. When the Internet first began in the 1980s and 1990s, users mostly used message boards and they are still a popular way to share information today. Message boards are usually integrated into particular website as a feature. For example, the movie and television information website imdb.com (Internet movie database) has message boards on each page; that is, for each movie or program they have a database page about, and for every actor, actress, or other motion picture professional. This lets users have a very specific place to say, discuss Joan Crawford's films overall or her acting in just a particular film, such as *Mildred Pierce*. Message boards are also invaluable when it comes to troubleshooting a product (Why is my Frigidaire refrigerator model XGBRG12 leaking water? How can I connect to WiFi on a Galaxy Tab 2?) because the content is usually totally open to anyone can post. Asking questions on a message board (such as, how do I know if my jade plant is ready to prune and repot?) is called crowdsourcing, but a user is trying to "source" their answer from the great crowd online, rather than from a particular, trusted source. (Note, too, that you should always take the advice and information offered on message boards with a grain of salt. The key to trusting information on a message board is repetition: if many users have said the same or similar things, the advice tends to be more trustworthy.)

Memes

Meme is a word that refers to anything that has spread around the Internet. These are often jokes, news stories that are sometimes hoaxes or sometimes just small news stories that have been magnified and have reached millions, or funny/shocking/surprising images. Most memes are fake or meant to be artificial; these can include something such as a shocking picture of a giant shark leaping out of the water to attack someone being lifted out of the ocean by a helicopter, or small children holding very large rabbits that seem to be as big as they are. Often, Internet users, especially inexperienced Internet users, have trouble telling that these things are hoaxes. A meme can be anything shared around social networking sites or via email. Recent examples of popular memes are endless variations of the slogan "keep calm and carry on," such as "keep calm and eat bacon" or "keep calm and kill zombies"; endless variations and remixes of people "twerking" like Myley Cyrus, or cute pictures of cats with funny taglines. By the time this reaches you, those things will be long out of fashion as trending memes.

Going "Viral"

When a meme—or any Internet content (news story, image, blog posting, quotation, tweet, etc.)—is so widely shared that it seems to be everywhere online, being endlessly reblogged, reposted on Facebook, retweeted, and so on, it is said to have gone "viral," as in, it has "infected" the entire Internet. For marketers—or celebrities or politicians—going viral is a goal because it means that people will click on and read your content without you having to pay for advertisements. A recent post on cracked.com, though, posited that going viral will mean much less going forward than it has in the recent Internet post. That article "4 Reasons 'Viral' Content Stopped Mattering in 2013" (http://www.cracked.com/blog/4-reasons-viral-content-stopped-mattering-in-2013/) makes the argument that the hyperbole expressed in most viral content sets up false expectations and ultimately disappoints readers with outrageous headlines that don't match actual content. While the concept of virality or "reach" (how many users see a particular post or article) will remain with us, it does make sense that popular content, as it is posted and reposted hundreds or thousands of times, will keep showing up almost anywhere online. So instead of "virality," perhaps a model of "infestation" works better. The content is in so many places that it does not need to catch like a virus. The article on cracked is useful and interesting to check out because it contains many examples of "viral" content you can share with beginning Internet users. See additional activities mentioned later in this chapter for tips.

Internet and Message Board Slang

Even advanced Internet users are sometimes thrown off by slang. Message boards tend to develop their own cultures, socially and linguistically, and users should be prepared to sometimes puzzle over what they are reading. Users will abbreviate whenever they can, especially if the conversation in the message board/discussion forum has been going for a while. To that end, users should be ready to figure out some slang terms. Here are a few that are useful for message boards:

IRL = in real life, as in "would you ever say that to me IRL" or "do you want to meet IRL"
IMHO = in my humble opinion or IMO=in my opinion, as in "IMHO Scarlett Johanssen is the worst actress" or "IMO, Vermont has the best skiing in New England"
ROFL = rolling on the floor laughing, as in: "when that cat jumped out of the vending machine, [I was] ROFL"
LOL = laugh out loud, as in: "look at the crazy eyes on that member of Congress decrying witchcraft in schools, LOL" (Historically, this also meant "lots of love" or "lots of luck," but now is pretty exclusively "laugh out loud" online.)
tl;dr = too long, didn't read (as in, this blog post was too long and I didn't read it)
btw = by the way

Sharing Events

There are web services built just for inviting people to real-life events. Two common ones are Evite and Eventbrite. In addition, Facebook has a robust event feature that allows users to input the time, place, and other information about an event and then invite users. When planning any kind of event, from a library friends group fundraiser or poetry slam to a kid's first birthday party or even a wedding, an online invitation is a quick and cheap way to doing the invitations. These services also let the event creator track who has read the invitation, who has responded yes, no, or maybe, and there are also commenting functions built in so users can say what kind of dish they are bringing to the potluck, for example. To create and publicize an event with these services, users need to be registered account holders at the site in question. And while you can pick whether or not the event is public or private, users should be aware that using public invites via email, social networking, or other event sharing space could offer less privacy than mailing paper invitations to someone's house.

COMMON ERRORS AND HOW TO SOLVE THEM

This workshop is potentially embarrassing to users and instructors alike, but remains one of the primary reasons people want to get online. Librarians should protect their own privacy by registering sample accounts and not showing their own profiles. In addition, be wary of users willing to offer you too much personal information about their dating history.

WORKSHOP PLAN

Remind participants of the discussion about "big data" from an earlier session or workshop. "Big data" refers to the massive amounts of statistics Internet companies keep and analyze based on the way Internet users browse, click, read, or play media online. Programs (or hackers) with access to the web histories and behaviors or hundreds of thousands or even millions of users can provide surprisingly specific and precise information about a user. Caution the class that when they share something online, such as posting something to Facebook, they are adding to the data about themselves available. Internet companies, such as Facebook, periodically change their terms of service and usually notify users that the terms of service have been updated. Many users do not notice these changes, and additionally, you have to accept the changes to keep using the service.

Explain that since the early days of the Internet, users have illegally traded music, video, and picture files. The name Napster might be familiar: this was a special web service set up to let individual Internet users all over the world upload the songs they owned for others to take and to download song files. Napster was closed down in 2001 by a court order that ruled the file sharing illegal. In addition, the copyright holders to some of the downloaded music sued individual users and received monetary settlements. Does that mean that no one illegally shares content they do not have the rights to? Of course not. But be sure the class participants are aware that sharing or distributing content that they do not have the rights to could open them up to legal or other trouble.

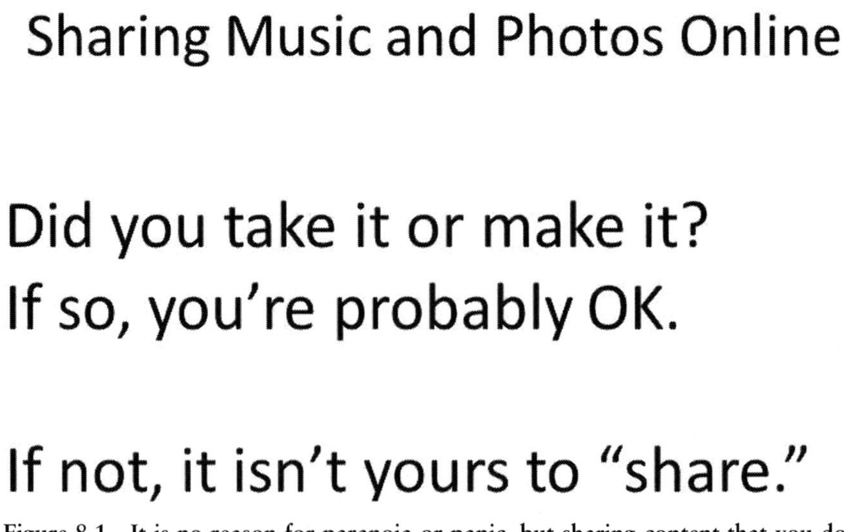

Sharing Music and Photos Online

Did you take it or make it?
If so, you're probably OK.

If not, it isn't yours to "share."

Figure 8.1   It is no reason for paranoia or panic, but sharing content that you do not own the rights to can expose you to legal risk.

The Digital Millenium Copyright Act (DMCA) makes it necessary to pay the copyright holders for electronic distribution and access.

Figure 8.2   Encourage interested users to search and learn more about the Digital Millennium Copyright Act (DMCA) and how it might affect their Internet use.

Tell participants that there ways to safely and legally share music and videos. There are many ways! But the most straightforward is convenient for beginning computer users is to share a link to their desired content, usually from YouTube. It would work like this: You want to post your aunt Andy's favorite song on her Facebook page for her birthday. So you search youtube.com for that song, either with an attached video or not. Then you post the link to that YouTube video on her page. This keeps you safe from the copyright police because any potential violation would be the problem of the original uploader to YouTube or of YouTube itself.

Even though we may not personally care that file sharing is illegal or find it ethically suspect, it is the law. This library's Internet use policy stipulates that all Internet use must be legal!

Inform students that the next topic they will learn about is Internet message boards. These are websites where one user starts a topic and then other users can post replies. Class members have probably already seen some versions of these, including Yahoo Answers. Message boards are great because they let users find very specific communities online.

Show the class how to get to imdb.com, the Internet movie database, by navigating there on your computer.

Explain that imbd.com is a great example of a message board because it has message boards integrated into every database entry.

Show users: Enter "Joan Crawford" in the search box, and click on "Joan Crawford (I) (1906–1977). Then scroll down. Near the very bottom is a link reading "Discuss Joan Crawford on the imdb message boards." Click it.

Navigate to imdb.com

Figure 8.3 Using screenshots such as this one is second best to using a live desktop you can project for workshop participants to watch.

Tell users that as they can see, this is a great place to really get specific with others who might have the same interest! As of this writing, there are almost 100 separate message board postings just about Joan Crawford, an actress who has been dead for almost 40 years.

Explain that message boards are also invaluable when it comes to troubleshooting a product (Why is my Frigidaire refrigerator model XGBRG12 leaking water? How can I connect to WiFi on a Galaxy Tab 2?) because the content is usually totally open and anyone can post. Asking questions on a message board (such as, how do I know if my jade plant is ready to prune and repot?) is called crowdsourcing, but a user is trying to "source" their answer from the great crowd online, rather than from a particular, trusted source.

Tell users that message boards are like the wild west of the Internet! It's uncensored, often out of control and can be very surprising. They tend to develop their own slang and conventions that can sometimes strike beginning users as odd or confusing. Give the class some examples of that slang.

Explain that one of the other important concepts to understand about social media sharing and message boards is memes. This is a general term that refers to widespread online. Memes are often jokes, news stories that are sometimes hoaxes, or sometimes just small news stories that have been magnified and have reached millions, or funny/shocking/surprising images. Most memes are fake or meant to be artificial; these include something such as a shocking picture of a giant shark leaping out of the water to attack someone being lifted out of the ocean by a helicopter, or small children holding very large rabbits that seem to be as big as they are. Often, Internet users, especially inexperienced Internet users, have trouble telling that these things are hoaxes. A meme can be anything shared around social networking sites or via email. Recent examples of popular memes are endless variations of

Crowdsourcing = asking the whole internet for help

(Like shouting "Does this look normal?" in a crowded theater.)

Figure 8.4   Use simplified and clear explanations of important terms and ideas. Keep in mind that many people with low digital literacy also have low levels of print literacy, as well.

Message Board Slang

IRL = in real life, as in "would you ever say that to me IRL" or "do you want to meet IRL"

IMHO = in my humble opinion or **IMO** = in my opinion, as in "IMHO Scarlett Johanssen is the worst actress" or "IMO, Vermont is the best skiing in New England"

ROFL = rolling on the floor laughing, as in: "when that cat jumped out of the vending machine, [i was] ROFL"

LOL = laugh out loud, as in: "look at the crazy eyes on that member of Congress decrying witchcraft in schools, LOL"

tl;dr = too long, didn't read (as in, this article was too long and I didn't read it)

Figure 8.5   Internet slang changes as fast or even faster than other kinds of language. Do not be afraid to Google an unfamiliar or confusing term.

the slogan "keep calm and carry on," such as "keep calm and eat bacon" or "keep calm and kill zombies"; endless variations and remixes of people "twerking" like Miley Cyrus or cute pictures of cats with funny taglines.

Ask the class if they have seen any examples of "memes." Which ones? Did they make sense to you?

Explain that the last thing you want to show the group about sharing and living online is how to host events. Many people use Facebook to create events and invite people to them. These could be private events such as baby showers or house warming parties, or public events such as marches or vigils.

Tell users if you already have a Facebook account, you can walk them through creating an event and inviting people. Ask them to navigate to Facebook.com and log in.

Point out that along the left-hand side of the page, under favorites, there is a link for events. Click it. This shows what events you may have already been invited to, via Facebook.

Tell participants that to create a new event, they can click the "+create event" button located at the top right of the page. This opens a dialogue box in the web page. They can then fill in the following information:

- Name of event
- Details
- Where
- When (date)
- When (time)
- Privacy: select from public, friends of guests, or invite only

Navigate to facebook.com

Figure 8.6 Even when navigating to well-known or common websites, beginning users need clear and explicit directions.

Not a Facebook user?

Try eventbrite.com

Figure 8.7 Even though mega sites such as Facebook or Twitter seem to have it all, there are excellent reasons to choose web services smaller in scope or offering just one function you need, such as electronic invitations and event management.

Explain that once they have filled out this information, they may also select the box for the option that "guests can invite their friends." Otherwise, the invitations will be limited to whom they select in the next step.

Ask students to click the blue "invite friends" link to send an invitation to this new event to anyone in their friends list. Then have them select the box next to their profile picture and name, or search (if you have too many to scroll through) by entering their name in the search blank at the top. To finish, they simply click the save button.

The page will then resolve to the event page. Explain that at this stage, they could add a photograph to accompany their invitation. Click "add event photo" to select one of your Facebook photos to use.

Two other invitation web services to tell the class about are evite.com and eventbrite.com. Explain that users must register at these two websites with a username/password, and need a valid email address. After a short registration, they can create events and enter email addresses of the people they want to invite. Each site has comprehensive "how to" guides, which they can access at:

http://help.eventbrite.com/customer/en_us/portal/articles/430478? [Google search string: "eventbrite how to"] for Eventbrite

http://evite.desk.com/ [Google search string "evite help"] for Evite.

HANDS-ON ACTIVITIES

A. Direct users to http://www.cracked.com/blog/4-reasons-viral-content-stopped-mattering-in-2013/ (Google search string "4 reasons viral content stopped mattering cracked.com"). Read this article and discuss examples of viral posts.

B. Remind users about the definition of "meme" and then direct them to http://knowyourmeme.com/memes/popular. Browse this site together and show examples. Ask users if they have experienced any versions of these memes or jokes, or if they have an idea for one they could make themselves.

C. Search for any message board results about a popular television show. Challenge participants to look at the one on imdb.com, but then also use Google to look for others.

D. Direct users to youtube.com, and ask them to search for a song they like. Then, direct them to highlight and copy the uniform resource locator (URL) for that YouTube video, and show them how to paste it into an email to share or onto a social media platform or message board.

9

Building and Sustaining
Digital Literacy Instruction
in Your Library

GETTING STARTED

If your library is already offering some kind of computer instruction, attempt to schedule the sessions regularly and repeat computer basics workshops often. While many Americans are using the Internet at home, millions still have no access except in a public library. Be sure to print up paper collateral—flyers, calendars, and other brochures—to have available for users to pick up and to use in outreach. It may take multiple contacts—a flyer, a verbal invitation, a phone call reminder, or multiple outreach visits to a senior center or transitional housing facility—before someone decides to come to a computer basics class and can actually come in the library at the right time. In my experience, it sometimes takes several weeks or a month of just one or two participants before enough word of mouth spreads (and your other advertising and outreach reaches) widely.

Survey your library patrons formally or informally and determine what times of day and days of the week are best for them, and adapt your schedules accordingly. If you have a computer lab, classroom space, or a laptop cart, of course make use of them for this kind of instruction, or use these programs to help write proposals or grants that would get you a lab or laptop cart. But even if you have to teach computer basics on the floor of the library, with everyone bringing their own laptop or using the library's public PCs, do it! These skills are vital and computer basics training can be even more effectively delivered one-on-one or one-on-two, if you do not have access to a lab or classroom space.

LIBRARY WEBSITE AND CATALOGUE AS LEARNING TOOL

Consider embedding computer basics information, training or practice modules, and other courseware links into your library website. That way, anyone looking for help from home or another location has an additional access point available. The website should have your calendar and descriptions of the computer basics classes so other agencies and interested parties can effectively refer potential learners.

In the hands-on activities time in the workshops, and during other open practice time, consider designing short tours of the library website. This should include searching the catalogue, accessing and searching the electronic resources and other databases, placing holds or requests, reviewing, tagging or making lists of library materials (if your OPAC has those functions), or subscribing to and commenting on the library blog or social media pages. Many library websites are goldmines of local resource information, from history and genealogy to social service referral and literacy building. Remember that bridging the digital divide has to be about more than teaching people to point and click, or to register email address they will never use. The more you can connect your learners and library patrons to necessary and useful online communities, information, and experiences, the more motivated they will be use and master the Internet.

RECRUITING, TRAINING, AND MOTIVATING OTHER INSTRUCTORS

Teaching computer basics day after day and week after week can be a slog for some librarians and library workers. Often it is an additional task someone has volunteered for or been assigned to, and comes with all the other programming, reference, and administrative duties they already have. Teaching people with low levels of print and digital literacy can be slow and frustrating work, and you will find yourself teaching the same set of skills over and over again. Refresh your practice and share the work by recruiting and training other staff members. If you are in a supervisory role, consider making it part of a rotating assignment where different staff members share the teaching responsibility on different days or different weeks.

Of course use this book at a training resource, but also be sure to train additional trainers through observation and participation. That means that a librarian or other staff member should sit in on and participate in one or more computer basics workshops before helming one on their own. In addition, schedule frequent check-in meetings where librarians and other library working engaged with digital literacy instruction can meet to discuss challenges, propose innovations, and solve problems collaboratively. Remember that computer instruction is a kind of library programming! Staff should offer it as frequently and as fundamentally as storytime.

Because this work can be frustrating, it is important to acknowledge and appreciate it when your staff or coworkers teach computer basics. Be sure to show that you listening to concerns, helping to solve problems, and seeking more and more support for digital literacy instructors. Encourage them to share their experiences on twitter. These hashtags will help find relevant content from other librarians working in digital literacy: #libchat, #digilit, #libtech. In addition, make this kind of a work an explicit part of professional development, by seeking out webinars and by attending programs and conferences to learn what other libraries are doing. Check the conference listings of your state or province's library and educational associations, the American Library Association, Public Library Association, Computers in Libraries, among others.

CENTERING ON THE COMMUNITY AND ON YOUR USER

Every library user who might end up in a computer basics class will need an email address, but otherwise, expect a diverse group with diverse needs and interests. In addition, your community's needs and interests should guide your computer basics instruction. Use demonstrated and anecdotal interests to improve your digital literacy instruction and to make it more relevant. If your community is largely job seekers, consider embedding job seeking skills into all the workshops from the most basic onward by making all the sites you visit together in class job search sites or pages with interview tips, resume examples, and so on. If you are in a city or region with lots of passion for local sports teams, include their websites, local commentary, how to find game schedules, or how to connect with the team or players on social media. If your computer basics crowd also contains members of your book club, be sure to show them how to find author and publisher websites, video or audio interviews, book trailers or blogs, among others. The point is that the more relevant online information is to your computer basics learners, the more they will put into their experience in the workshop.

PATIENCE AND PRACTICE

The learners in your computer basics class will also need frequent reminders that the tasks they are undertaking are difficult, and that they are not "dumb" or unintelligent. Computers, tablets, phones, and devices have ways of making even the most tech savvy users feel stupid. I always remind computer basics learners over and over again that computers are "stupid" in the sense that they are very literal, and they are relying on input from a user to do anything. Bear in mind that using a mouse to navigate windows, links, menus, and buttons is a physical method of interacting with a completely abstract set of "things." For people with little context about how the Internet works and why it is relevant to them, these abstractions do not always make sense.

Always encourage your learners to be patient, with themselves, with the technology on offer, and with you and the rest of the class. Dozens of hours of computer instruction will not help on their own; encourage learners at your library to practice and practice, and make available more computer time for them whenever possible. Beginning users should expect to do some computer tasks dozens—or even hundreds—of times before they have created a confident pattern they can rely on.

ENCOURAGING SELF-GUIDED LEARNING

Appendix A lists several online courseware resources that users can access on their own from home or the library for extra practice. In addition, these same resources are available as a reproducible handout to distribute during your computer basics classes in Appendix C. These resources are great ways to practice the fundamentals covered in this guide. Be sure to make them available to your learners after a computer basics workshop. Consider posting them near the public access PCs, so beginning users who are not in a class might also access them.

If you are running a workshop series, you can offer light homework tasks based on the hands-on activities described here. Enhance them with topics of local interest, and ask learners to complete very basic tasks, such as: Send your daughter an email before class meets again, collect up to three URLs (uniform resource locators) from television commercials to investigate, find out how old the president is, and so on. The more charge a computer basics learner can take of their own learning, the richer and more rewarding these classes will be for them, and for you as the instructor.

Appendix A

Free Online Courseware
for Computer Basics

Recommend these websites and resources as additional practice for your workshop participants and use them to support independent online learning in the library and at home. Consider posting this information on your library website as an at-home learning resource for people who are visiting your "electronic" branch only.

GCF Learn Free | http://www.gcflearnfree.org/computers [Google search terms: GCF learn free]

This site is a program of Goodwill Industries, and contains many tutorials in subjects ranging from computer basics and typing tutorial to iPad basics, social media, and even more advanced topics such as Microsoft Access. The tutorials consist of lessons, interactives, videos, and extras to help users learn and practice computer and Internet skills.

BBC WebWise | http://www.bbc.co.uk/webwise/courses/computer-basics/ [Google search terms: BBC webwise]

Produced by the British Broadcasting Company, this website of video tutorials feature outgoing personalities and professionally produced video content. The subject areas offered on WebWise are "your computer," "using the web," "email & sharing," "living & interests," and "safety & privacy," and there is also a helpful glossary of terms. In addition, the "courses" link pulls these various content areas into four courses: "The WebWise Online Course," "Internet Basics," "Computer Basics," and "Social Media Basics."

Microsoft Digital Literacy: Basic Curriculum | https://www.microsoft.com/about/corporatecitizenship/citizenship/giving/programs/up/digitalliteracy/eng/Basic Curriculum.mspx [Google search terms: Microsoft digital literacy]

This offering from the world's largest PC software manufacturer and the most widely used Internet browser (Internet Explorer) is not as clear or easy to understand as other online course modules. But it does offer very comprehensive (if sometimes out of date) tutorials on Microsoft software products.

Basic Online Skills (for the Connecticut Distance Learning Consortium) | https:// www.ctdlc.org/remediation/ [Google search terms: ctdlc basic online skills]

This site features simple and straightforward text-based and interactive tutorials in four broad areas: computer skills, email skills, Word processing skills, and web skills. Because there are no videos that need high-speed connections or sound amplification, they are ideal for a library environment. The mouse over- view (https://www.ctdlc.org/remediation/mouse.html) is very useful for first- time users who have never used a mouse device to navigate a computer screen before.

Free Library Hot Spots Wiki How to Videos | http://hotspots.freelibrary.wikispaces .net/How-to+Videos [Google search terms: flp hot spots wiki]

This site, from the Free Library of Philadelphia, features six how-to videos on topics such as "How to sign up for a Gmail account" or "How to use Google Maps to find directions." Although there are only a few videos, they are comprehensive, authoritative, and practical. In addition, they are designed for computer beginners with low levels of literacy.

Appendix B

Bibliography and Additional Resources

PRINT

Bertot, John Carlo, et al. *Public Libraries and the Internet: Roles, Perspectives, and Implications.* Santa Barbara: Libraries Unlimited, 2011.

Grassian, Esther, et al. *Information Literacy Instruction: Theory and Practice.* 2nd ed. (*Information Literacy Sourcebook*). Chicago: Neal-Schuman Publishers, Inc., 2009.

Kirchhoff, Liz M. *Teaching Social Media: The Can-Do Guide.* Santa Barbara: Libraries Unlimited, 2014.

McFedries, Paul *Teach Yourself VISUALLY Computers.* 5th ed. Hoboken: Wiley, 2011.

Miller, Michael. *Computer Basics Absolute Beginner's Guide.* 6th ed. Indianapolis, IN: Que, 2012.

Sittler, Ryan L., and Douglas Cook. *The Library Instruction Cookbook.* Chicago: ACRL, 2009.

West, Jessamyn C. *Without a Net: Librarians Bridging the Digital Divide.* Santa Barbara: Libraries Unlimited, 2011.

White, Ron. *How Computers Work.* Upper Saddle River: Que, 2007.

Yelton, Andromeda. *Bridging the Digital Divide with Mobile Services.* Chicago: ALA Editions, 2012.

WEB

Becket, Stefan. "The 2013 Twitter Glossary: Tabs, Hatereads, Doge, and More." *New York Magazine* online edition. Published December 31, 2013. http://nymag .com/daily/intelligencer/2013/12/2013-twitter-glossary-doge-hatereads-tabs-mansplain-meaning.html.

"Evaluating Web Pages: Techniques to Apply and Questions to Ask." UC Berkeley, Teaching Library Internet Workshops. 2012. http://www.lib.berkeley.edu/ TeachingLib/Guides/Internet/Evaluate.html.

"Resources to Search the Invisible Web." Perdue University Online Writing Lab. https://owl.english.purdue.edu/owl/resource/558/07/.

Schwartz, Barry. "Google: Duplicate Content Pollutes 25–30% of the Web." Search Engine Roundtable. December 17, 2013. http://www.seroundtable.com/google-web-duplicate-17827.html.

"The Ultimate Guide to the Invisible Web." Open Education Database. http://oedb .org/ilibrarian/invisible-web/.

"Web Literacy Standard." Mozilla Foundation. http://webmaker.org/standard and https://wiki.mozilla.org/Learning/WebLiteracyStandard.

Appendix C

Sample Handouts

FREE ONLINE COURSEWARE HANDOUT

Keep learning and practicing at home with these free websites. Either type in the web address exactly as it appears below or use a search engine (such as Google) with the suggested phrase to find the site.

GCF Learn Free |
http://www.gcflearnfree.org/computers
[Google search terms: GCF learn free]

BBC WebWise |
http://www.bbc.co.uk/webwise/courses/computer-basics/
[Google search terms: BBC webwise]

Microsoft Digital Literacy: Basic Curriculum |
https://www.microsoft.com/about/corporatecitizenship/citizenship/
giving/programs/up/digitalliteracy/eng/BasicCurriculum.mspx
[Google search terms: Microsoft digital literacy]

Basic Online Skills (for the Connecticut Distance Learning
Consortium) |
https://www.ctdlc.org/remediation/
[Google search terms: ctdlc basic online skills]

Free Library Hot Spots Wiki How to Videos |
http://hotspots.freelibrary.wikispaces.net/How-to+Videos
[Google search terms: flp hot spots wiki]

From *Teaching Internet Basics: The Can-Do Guide* by Joel A. Nichols. Santa Barbara, CA: Libraries Unlimited. Copyright © 2014.

SIX MOST IMPORTANT KEYS

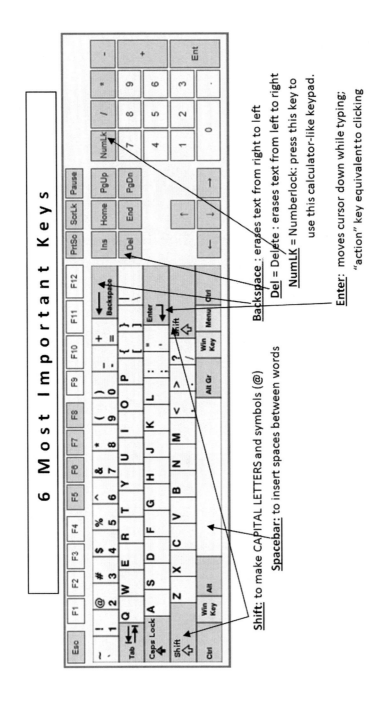

Figure AppC.1   Sample handout showing the six most important keys on a keyboard.

SAMPLE MOUSE 101 HANDOUT

Holding the Mouse:

- Put the heel of your hand on the desk just below the mouse.
- Rest the palm of your hand on the hump of the mouse and hold the mouse between your thumb and ring finger.
- Rest your index finger on the left mouse button, your middle finger on the right mouse button.
- Be sure to keep the mouse on a flat and smooth surface.

Moving the Mouse:

- Use your elbow and not your wrist. Keep the wrist straight and firm and pivot at the elbow.
- Keep the mouse on the flat and smooth surface. If the mouse is lifted, the cursor will stop following the movement.
- **Most importantly, do not turn the mouse!**

Clicking:

- The cursor will change from an arrow to a pointer when it is over a clickable object.
- The left button will do most of the work. Keep your index finger on it (do not suspend your finger above it).
- When clicking, press your index finger down until you hear a click and ease up until you are resting on the button again.
- To double click, press your index finger down twice rapidly. Keep your finger on the button (do not lift your finger into the air).
- Right click has other functions, such as copying, cutting, and pasting.

Dragging and Dropping:

- Place cursor over the object you wish to drag.
- Press your index finger down and hold it.
- Move the mouse while your finger is in this position. The object will follow under the cursor.
- To "drop" the object, release your index finger.

Radio Buttons and Checkboxes:
- These are often found in multiple choice and checklist settings
- Radio buttons :

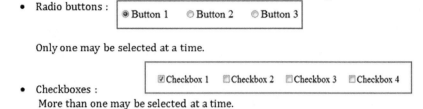

Only one may be selected at a time.

- Checkboxes :
More than one may be selected at a time.

Drop-Down Menus:
Click on the downward facing arrow to the right.

Scrolling:
- **There several ways to do this.**
- Click and hold the <u>top arrow</u> to scroll up and the <u>bottom arrow</u> to scroll down.
- Place the cursor on the <u>bar</u> and drag up or down.
- Use the wheel

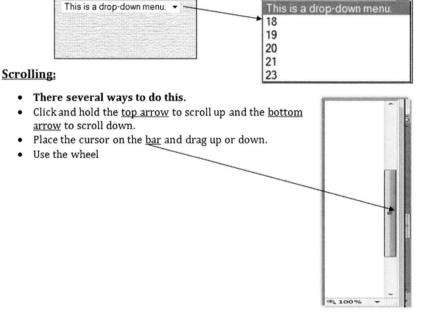

Practice Sites:

http://www.ckls.org/~crippel/computerlab/tutorials/mouse/page1.html

Google search terms: Mousercise, Mouserobics, Mouse tutorial

Figures AppC.2 and App C.3   Sample handouts should use lots of white space to be clear to low-literacy populations, but should also strive to act as a resource new users can rely on for practice by themselves.

From *Teaching Internet Basics: The Can-Do Guide* by Joel A. Nichols. Santa Barbara, CA: Libraries Unlimited. Copyright © 2014.

HOW TO BUY A COMPUTER: SOME TIPS

Computers—What to look for when you go to buy.

There are three main variables when purchasing a computer: *RAM*, *CPU*, and *hard drive*. Here are some general *guidelines*:

RAM (random access memory): The more RAM you have, the faster your computer will run and the more programs/windows you can have open at once. You probably want at least 2 GB (gigabytes) of RAM, and should not need more that 4 GB.

CPU (central processing unit): Ideally, you want above 3 gigahertz. However, 2.5 to 2.8 is fine for most home computing.

Hard drive: This is the long-term memory storage your computer will use. At least 160 GB will do, but many newer computers come with as much as 300. If you are interested in storing large amounts of music, video, or photographs on your computer, you may want a larger hard drive.

**RAM is what will make your computer's performance better. If you are playing around with price, and can afford more/faster/larger of one of the above, chose *RAM*.

**Be sure you know *how your computer will connect to the Internet.* This will probably mean in-home WiFi or personal 4G hotspot device. Also, remember:

- Be skeptical. The person selling the computer is trying to get the most money from you, not give you the best computer for your needs or budget.
- Desktop PCs are cheaper than laptops, and tend to last longer. Be sure read the fine print: is there a monitor included in the price? How long is the manufacturer warranty, and so on?
- Beware of extra warranties that cost too much. Most computers will come with a limited warranty that covers the machine for a year or so. Often, those extra plans end up costing more than buying a replacement PC would.
- Most software applications you want should come free with the computer. Think twice before purchasing anything extra until you know what you need.
- Shop around and wait for a deal.
- Read for yourself: ask the librarian to show you the books about buying or operating personal computers. Often, the first chapters of these books about computers will have buying tips.

From *Teaching Internet Basics: The Can-Do Guide* by Joel A. Nichols. Santa Barbara, CA: Libraries Unlimited. Copyright © 2014.   127

MONTHLY CALENDAR (BILINGUAL) AND SAMPLE WORKSHOP DESCRIPTIONS

COMPUTER LAB SCHEDULE | HORARIO DEL LABORATORIO DE COMPUTACIÓN

April | Abril

Tuesday	Wednesday	Thursday	Friday	Saturday
6 1-2: Open Lab 3-7: Teen Lab	7 2-6: Open Lab	8 10-1:30 Open Lab 3-5: Teen Lab	9 2-5: Open Lab	10 10-11: Computer Basics 11-12: Clase Básica 12-1: Internet Basics 1-5: Open Lab
13 12-4: Open Lab	14 2-6: Open Lab	15 10-1:30 Open Lab 3-5: Teen Lab	16 10-5: Open Lab	17 10-11: Computer Basics 11-12: Clase Básica 12-1: Micrsoft Word 1-5: Open Lab
20 1-2: Open Lab 3-7: Teen Lab	21 2-6: Open Lab	22 10-1:30 Open Lab 3-5: Teen Lab	23 2-5: Open Lab	24 10-11: Computer Basics 11-12: Clase Básica 12-1: Powerpoint 1-5: Open Lab
27 1-2: Open Lab 3-7: Teen Lab	28 2-6: Open Lab	29 10-1:30 Open Lab 3-5: Teen Lab	30 2-5: Open Lab	

All classes are first come, first served. Schedule is subject to change.
Las clases no son reservadas y no necesita registrarse El horario es susceptible al cambio

Lillian Marrero Branch | Sucursal Lillian Marrero
Free Library of Philadelphia | Biblioteca Publica de Filadelfia
601 West Lehigh Avenue (6th & Lehigh)
Philadelphia, PA 19133-2228
215-685-9794
www.freelibrary.org

Figure AppC.4 Offer a master monthly calendar with all computer and digital literacy workshops in one place. This makes it easy for patrons—and staff—to find out when you are offering computer classes.

From *Teaching Internet Basics: The Can-Do Guide* by Joel A. Nichols. Santa Barbara, CA: Libraries Unlimited. Copyright © 2014.

In addition, here are some sample course descriptions and other language for your flyers and calendars in English and Spanish.

All classes are first come, first served. Schedule is subject to change.

Computer Classes

Computer Basics: Learn to use the keyboard and mouse and register yourself an email account.
Every Tuesday at 11 A.M. and Saturday at 10 A.M.

Job Hunters' Workshop: Write, revise, type, and print your resume and get help filling out job applications.
Every Thursday at 10 A.M.

Microsoft Word: Prepare yourself for school or work by learning the basics of this word processing program, including typing, saving a file, spell check, spacing, among others.
Every Friday at 10 A.M.

Las clases no son reservadas y no necesita registrarse. El horario es susceptible al cambio Clases de Computación

Clase básica de computación: Aprenda como usar el teclado, el ratón y cómo registrarse en una cuenta de correo electrónico, completamente gratis.
Todos los martes a las 11 A.M. y los sábados a las 10 A.M.

Taller de búsqueda de empleo por Internet: Prepare, escriba, revise su curriculum viate y obtenga ayuda personalizada para llenar sus aplicaciones de trabajo online.
Todos los jueves a las 10 A.M.

Microsoft Word: Prepárese para la escuela o el trabajo aprendiendo como usar el programa de procesamiento de textos.
Todos los viernes a las 10 A.M.

Reproducible Glossary
of Key Concepts

Attachments: Since the body of an email can really only hold text and textual information, other kinds of files can be sent along with an email as an attachment. Almost any kind of file can be attached to an email and then sent to an intended recipient, although email services (both server client and webmail) usually have a size limit for attachments. The most common forms of an attachment are documents, picture or photo files, or sometimes music or video. (The last two are less common because they usually require much larger file sizes, but users will find that people sometimes do send short videos or sound files as attachments.)

Billing Address: Online stores will also want a billing address, or the address that belongs to your credit/debit card account. Sometimes, this will be the same as the shipping address, and to that end, most online retailers offer a box users can click that says "same as shipping address."

Bold, Italic, and Underline: Three other basic and standard text formatting options exist, and should already be familiar to even a beginning user. They are:

1. Bold
2. Italic
3. Underline

Browsers: Browsers are software programs that translate computer code into words, pictures, music, and video. Browsers are the primary way that we humans, and especially we humans in this class, will interact with web pages.

Checking Out: When users are ready to purchase the items they have selected, they will need to click a link that says "checkout" or "purchase," just as they would have to bring their purchases up to a cash register in a bricks and mortar store. There is usually a checkout link (which might say "buy" or "purchase") on every page of the store, usually near the top of the page. In addition, the shopping cart itself usually has a larger button or link near the bottom of the page for checking out. Once a user clicks "checkout" the store either (1) requires them to log in to an account or (2) allows them to checkout as a guest and brings them to the forms where they will fill out their shipping address, their billing address, pick from a variety of shipping speeds and methods, and also enter their payment information.

Comments and Message Boards: Another way people share ideas and information online are via comments and message boards. Most blogs offer commenting facility, and so do many news websites and other services. Thousands—or even millions at this point—of web services have also integrated Facebook commenting into their sites, so users can actually use their Facebook accounts to comment on a given Internet web link or news story. Some blogs and sites allow users to post a comment anonymously, although being able to maintain anonymity is harder and harder as more sites require a username/login to post.

Composing Email/Writing a New Message: One of the primary functions of having an email account is being able to write and send emails. In various webmail services, users will find a button or link that says "compose" or "new message" or "write new email." When users click that button, a new blank message form will pop up. This form will have several blank fields for users to fill out. The most important of these are (1) the "to:" field, (2) the "subject:" field, and (3) the "message" field where the actual email goes.

Coupons and Promotions: Online retailers market aggressively, and usually have special promotions and coupons that users can use. Sometimes, previous shoppers (that is, registered users at a given online retailer) will receive emails with special offers. To redeem those special offers, there is often a code to be used at checkout.

Creative Commons Licenses: In response to closed copyright, a movement to offer licensed content that users can download for free, remix, and adulterate, as well as share more widely themselves has sprung up: creative commons. This is a kind of copyright license that lets content creators stipulate exactly what users can do with their content (text, photographs, music, or video) for free and without asking permission. These licenses provide a great way to learn about fair use and other copyright issues. Their mission is to build an infrastructure of content and rules for that content in order to maximize users' potential to creatively engage and share with other artistic and creative endeavors. Users making and posting their own web content should investigate realizing it under a creative commons license. The website has an easy to use tool that helps users select a license. Users must decide, for example, if they will let others modify their work in anyway, and if they will allow any commercial use of their work. It also stipulates very clearly how the work should be attributed to the creator to help make sure others are not passing off someone else's work as their own.

Credibility: The Internet is so diverse and powerful precisely because anyone can contribute content and information on web pages, blogs, or message boards. As a result, though, there is very little authority control. This can result in (1) inaccurate information or (2) unverified information. Users learning to search online need to be introduced to the concept of credibility, and should learn how to be prepared to find and recognize trusted sources.

From *Teaching Internet Basics: The Can-Do Guide* by Joel A. Nichols. Santa Barbara, CA: Libraries Unlimited. Copyright © 2014.

Deep Web or Hidden Web: Search engines scan the text of web pages, looking for and indexing keywords. But a lot of the content of the Internet lurks below the surface, much of it in databases. These databases are full of information that, when queried, serve up dynamic web pages to Internet users. This is important because it means that there are millions of web pages that virtually *do not exist* until a user is looking for them.

Digital Millennium Copyright Act (DMCA) and Digital Rights Management (DRM): Beginning Internet users often assume that everything is available online, and that everything is available for free online. While there are many sites where users can illegally access (via download) almost any content they desire, from Hollywood blockbuster movies to eBooks and whole albums, most of the legal ways of accessing music and video content cost money. They cost in part because the DMCA makes it necessary to pay the copyright holders for accessed materials.

Directories: Directories, another special kind of web page, list links to other web pages based on subject. They differ from search engines in that, rather than being categorized based on keywords and text matches, they are sorted instead by subject or category. The big search engine Yahoo used to function entirely as a directory, for example, offering users subject categories with many subheadings as a way to find other web pages.

Document Settings: When users want the same styles to apply to their entire text, or they want to modify attributes such as line spacing, space between paragraphs, size of margins, and so on, they will access the document settings or formatting settings. In Word, these are called document settings and are found under the page layout menu

Documents: When you use a computer to type information and want to save that text and information to later retrieval, to attach to email to send someone, or print out, you are generating a file called a document. The most common form of computer document is a file with the extension .docx, and it is the most common because that is standard Microsoft Word format.

Domain Names: The .com shows us that it is a commercial website. This suffix is an example of what is called a domain; other domains can show that a site is an educational site (.edu), a nonprofit organization (.org), or that it is a site from a country outside the United States (.co.uk for the United Kingdom or .jp for Japan).

Email: Email stands for electronic mail. It is designed to emulate "snail" or post-office mail in a digital environment, and enables users to send and receive private information online. To send and receive, users need an email account or an email address.

Email Addresses: Email addresses are much more like phone numbers in that they are a way to reach a specific person or individual. Distinguishing between email addresses and web addresses is as easy as the @ symbol. If an address has an @, it's an email address. If not, it's probably a web address.

File Types: There are almost as many file types as there are kinds of computer or tablet or smartphone, and sometimes users have trouble understanding when to use which one.

- .rtf, or rich-text format: These are plain and generic text files that can be opened by a variety of different word processing files. They do not feature rich formatting options, and are perfect for someone sending a file when they are not sure exactly how the person they are sending it to will open it.

- .txt, for text file: This is another plain text file with no formatting. These can be hard for users to work with because they often do not feature automatic text wraparound at the end of line.

- .pdf, or portable document format: This file type is a proprietary but standard way of sending "frozen" documents, or ones not able to be edited. Because all word processors format files differently based on system defaults, any .rtf or .docx might not display the way a user intended on a different machine or when printed out. Using .pdf format ensures that your document is saved and later displayed in exactly the format a user intended. (*Note:* For advanced users, note that there are some .pdfs with editable fields meant to be filled out and saved. These are often forms, so the form blanks will be editable but the rest of the text will not be. Note also that any .pdf will be editable using the proprietary Adobe Professional application.)

Font and Font Size: Word processing programs let users pick what they want their text to look like and are highly customizable. One of the ways users customize text is by changing the font or typeface or the size. Most word processing programs come with various styles to choose from, and there are thousands of fonts available for download and use. "Normal" printed text is usually between 10 and 14 points.

Going "Viral": When a meme—or any Internet content (news story, image, blog posting, quotation, tweet, etc.)—is so widely shared that it seems to be everywhere online, being endlessly reblogged, reposted on Facebook, retweeted, and so on, it is said to have gone "viral," as in, it has "infected" the entire Internet. For marketers—or celebrities or politicians—going viral is a goal because it means that people will click on and read your content without you having to pay for advertisements.

Hashtags on Twitter, Facebook, and Instagram: A relatively new way of finding information based on subject has emerged on Twitter and Instagram. When people post Facebook status updates or send tweets, they often include a subject term marked with a hashtag (#). Then, users can search all of Twitter, for example, for other tweets that have that same hashtag.

Inbox: An email inbox is where a user can find his or her email. New messages are always delivered to the inbox, and will stay in an inbox until users move them. Inbox interfaces are usually set up so users can see (1) who sent the message, (2) what the subject of an email is, and (3) a preview (the first few lines) of the email message itself.

Internet and Message Board Slang: Even advanced Internet users are sometimes thrown off by slang. Message boards tend to develop their own cultures, socially and linguistically, and users should be prepared to sometimes puzzle over what they are reading. Users will abbreviate whenever they can, especially if the conversation in the message board/discussion forum has been going for a while.

From *Teaching Internet Basics: The Can-Do Guide* by Joel A. Nichols. Santa Barbara, CA: Libraries Unlimited. Copyright © 2014.

IRL=in real life, as in "would you ever say that to me IRL" or "do you want to meet IRL"
IMHO=in my humble opinion; or IMO=in my opinion, as in "IMHO Scarlett Johanssen is the worst actress" or "IMO, Vermont has the best skiing in New England"
ROFL=rolling on the floor laughing, as in "when that cat jumped out of the vending machine, [I was] ROFL"
LOL=laugh out loud, as in "look at the crazy eyes on that member of Congress decrying witchcraft in schools, LOL" (Historically, this also meant "lots of love" or "lots of luck," but now is pretty exclusively "laugh out loud" online)
tl;dr=too long, didn't read, as in "this blog post was too long and I didn't read it"
Btw=by the way

Justification: In documents, text is justified to the left, to the center, or to the right, which means that the edge of the text is lined up against the right side of the page, the left side of the page, or down the middle.

Line Spacing: In documents, "line spacing" refers to the amount of whitespace in between lines of text. There are many options, but the most common are "single," "1.5," and "double." Single spacing fits more text on one page, but the lines are closer together.

Links: Links are the way we describe ways to get from one web page to another. When people make web pages, they create links that go from one page to the next. Remember, the Internet is made up of web pages. Links are ways to travel from one to the next, and are often typographically indicated with blue text or underlined text.

Memes: Meme is a word that refers to anything that has spread around the Internet. These are often jokes, news stories that are sometimes hoaxes or sometimes just small news stories that have been magnified and have reached millions, or funny/shocking/surprising images.

Password Recovery: Often, users will remember their usernames but not their passwords. Most sites have a link on the login page or near the username/password blanks that says something along the lines of "to reset password click here" or "forgot password? click here." When users click the link, they are taken to a password-recovery form where they need to enter their username or email address. Then, the website in question will send them via email either (1) a new password or (2) a link they must click from their email to bring them back to the website in question to reset the password.

Payment Options: The most common way to pay for something online is by using a credit or debit card. Users must provide their full credit card number, their billing zip code, and usually also the three-digit security code on the back of the card. Another common form of payment is PayPal (see below).

From *Teaching Internet Basics: The Can-Do Guide* by Joel A. Nichols. Santa Barbara, CA: Libraries Unlimited. Copyright © 2014.

PayPal: PayPal is an online payment service owned by the online retailer eBay, but users can use PayPal to pay for a variety of online goods and services. PayPal is a third-party service, meaning that it does not belong to the online retailer in question. Some users prefer this method, especially if they are buying things from individuals or smaller online retailers and are concerned about giving out their credit card information. When using PayPal, only PayPal has the credit card or bank account information.

Phishing: Phishing (pronounced like "fishing") is a specific kind of email spam where unscrupulous scammers try and trick user into clicking harmful links or entering information such as their banking, email, or social media passwords. When this "phishing" emails arrive in a user's inbox, they often appear to be legitimate communications from a bank or social media service like Facebook. They emulate the art and design of these sites, and encourage users to click a link and enter personal information.

Private Messages: Because many online daters are rightly reluctant to share too much personal information too quickly, most dating websites have a private message feature for users to exchange written messages. These are like emails, except that they are sent via a user's social media account instead of by email address.

Profile: The cornerstone of online dating at many sites is to create a profile. This functions somewhat (and looks) like a social networking profile users may be familiar with from Facebook, but Internet daters must take care and preserve more privacy in a dating profile. Users should think twice before sharing personal information such as address, phone number, or even email in a dating profile, even less often than they appear on other social networking services.

Registering an Account or Checking out as a Guest: When a user wants to make online purchases, they are asked to provide the online store with a lot of information. This information typically includes billing and shipping information, including names and addresses, phone numbers, and credit/debit card information. Some online stores require users to create an account that can be used every time they shop. Other online stores allow users to checkout as a guest, and enter the information without having to create a username and login that they could use again.

Save vs. Save As: Users of desktop word processors such as Microsoft Word should learn to save their work early and often to avoid losing any typing, and also to practice giving documents names and putting them in locations that make them easy to retrieve for editing and attaching later. Save just saves the current information in the file at its present location. "Save as" becomes a better choice, because it forces users to confirm (and allows users to change) three attributes about the file:

1. The name
2. The location
3. The file format

Search Engines: Search engines are special websites made for searching for other web sites. Search engines send automated computer programs (called robots) all over the Internet, reading and indexing pages. Whatever a user inputs into the search field is called a "query." Different search engines rely on different methods to make sure that the websites/links they are delivering are relevant to the original query.

Security Questions: Most Internet accounts—which should be taken very broadly to mean any website or app where you have to log in—are secured with a username and password. If users have forgotten their username or password or both, most accounts can be reset via email. Some accounts are also secured with security questions. These are secret questions the user selects and writes answers to. Then, when the user is seeking to change or recover a forgotten password, they must provide the answers anew.

Selecting Text, Copying, and Pasting: First, users must highlight or select the text they seek to copy. To highlight, users should hover the cursor in front of or behind the text they want to copy. Then they should click the house button and hold down the left-click button. While holding down the button, users can drag the cursor up and down, right and left to until the text they want to select is highlighted, or surrounded by a shading.

Sending Email: Once users have put an addressee in the "to:" field, written a subject in the "subject:" field and composed the body of their email, they are ready to click "send" for the email to go. This is often a button labeled "send," but could be an icon or pictograph, depending on the webmail service you have chosen.

Sent Folder: Every email program and service automatically files a copy of any emails a user sends in a folder called "sent mail." Much like the inbox, this folder is part of the major geography of any email service and is a good way for users to practice "finding" emails. This folder is useful because it maintains a record of sent email, including intended addressee(s), time and date, any files that might attached, and so on.

Sharing Events: There are web services built just for inviting people to real-life events. Two common ones are Evite and Eventbrite. In addition, Facebook has a robust event feature that allows users to input the time, place, and other information about an event and then invite users. To create and publicize an event with these services, users need to be registered account holders at the site in question. And while you can pick whether or not the event is public or private, users should be aware that using public invites via email, social networking, or other event sharing space could offer less privacy than mailing paper invitations to someone's house.

Sharing Music: Users may be interested in sharing music. There are many ways to do this. They can email or attach music files such as MP3 files to posts on social media. This method works best if users own the rights to the music file in question. If not, another common way to share music is by posting a link from some streaming music or video file (such as a music video on YouTube, for example) to someone's social media feed. In addition, there are special social media websites and services that are designed just to connect users based on music. The most popular of these is called Spotify, and lets users listen to music for free and created shared playlists to send to others. Spotify is useful for beginning users because it is legal, and users do not need to worry about unintentionally violating the Digital Millennium Copyright Act.

Shipping Address: Online stores need to send shoppers their purchases. Users therefore need to fill out a form with their shipping addresses during check out.

Shopping Cart: Most online stores have a virtual shopping cart or basket that users can add items to. This lets users keep an item ready for later comparison or purchasing. Nearly all online shops have links in their product information that reads "add to basket" or "add to shopping cart."

Social Search: While hashtags on Facebook and Twitter represent one form of powerful social searching, there are also other tools that Internet users can use to find out what their friends and communities online are saying or do know about a particular issue. These search tools give more credence to a particular website based on whether it has been used or mentioned on social networking sites.

Spam or Junk Mail: Much like junk letters arriving at your door promising to lower your monthly payments or sell you magazine subscriptions and grant you a million-dollar sweepstakes, companies and individuals also use unsolicited email as a marketing and solicitation tool. These emails are often generated by computer programs and have no humans involved. These computer programs scour the Internet for individuals' email addresses and then send their junk mail indiscriminately.

Spell Check and Grammar Check: Most word processing programs include a spelling and/or grammar checking tool. The programs are using a predefined dictionary of words or concepts that might not encompass the words someone is using, or suggest that slang is spelled incorrectly. While spell check can be a useful tool for users, keep in mind that these programs are checking a specific dictionary that might not include the needed words. (*Note:* Advanced users can add words to the dictionary in Microsoft Word, which might be handy for certain proper nouns or other frequently used jargon.)

Strong Passwords: Strong passwords are hard to guess, appear to be a random collection of numbers, letters, and even punctuation, and also make use of uppercase and lowercase letters. Something like "bX57ut0p1A" is a lot harder to guess than "rover6284."

Subject Field: It is important to use the subject field when sending an email. Because new emails in one's inbox show the sender and the subject line most prominently, it is crucial to give your emails a subject. Users can type anything into the subject field, but it is worth stressing that subject lines that accurately reflect the content of the email are probably more likely to be seen, opened, and read.

Tabs and Tabbed Browsing: Browser windows can only show one website or web page at a time. You can open up multiple browser windows to use more than one website at once, but that makes the computer desktop crowded and confusing very quickly.

"To:" Field, Cc:, and Bcc: Emails work like paper letters in the sense that they are addressed to and sent to particular individuals. In addition, there are two other fields you can use for email addresses: "cc:," which stands for "carbon copy" and "bcc:," for "blind carbon copy." "Cc:" or "carbon copy" is the same as putting more than one email address in the "to;" field. When you enter an email address into the "bcc:" or "blind carbon copy" field, the person you are emailing will get a copy of the email, but they will not be able to see who else was copied on the email, that is, whom else you sent the email.

Trash or Deleted Items Folder: The third major "place" in an email account is the trash. This folder is where emails end up when a user deletes them from the inbox. The email is stored in the trash/deleted items folder. Depending on the email service in question, how long the deleted email remains available in this folder will vary. Some email services keep deleted items forever. Some prompt users to empty their trash folders when their email service runs out of space to store more emails, which deletes the message from a user's account forever.

Username Rules: Websites almost impose some rules on what a username consists of. There will likely be a limit on the number of characters allowed: often at least 6 or 8, and usually not more than 16–20 in total. In addition, they may require or disallow special characters such a punctuation or underscores. Usernames have to be unique, that is, you cannot pick something that someone else has already served.

Usernames and Email Addresses: Distinguishing between usernames and entire email addresses can be frustrating and unclear to beginning users. Usernames are the personal part of an address: firstnamelastname, or in my case, joelnichols. Some organizations, schools, or companies tend to use the same pattern for generating usernames, which might include firstname.lastname (joel.nichols), lastnamefirstinitial (nicholsj), firstinitiallastname (jnichols), among others. But the username is just one part of the address. A complete email address uses a username plus the @ symbol plus a domain name.

View and Zoom: Users can enlarge the view of their documents by adjusting the zoom (zooming in or zooming out). This feature is useful for seniors, young people, and users with vision limitations. It does not change the size of the words in the file (i.e., they would not print enlarged, or be viewed enlarged if opened via email attachment on another computer).

Web Addresses: Web addresses are the exact addresses (URL; uniform resource locator) of a specific web page out of the millions of pages out there. Internet users navigate by knowing specific web addresses or knowing how to search for them.

Web Pages: Web pages are how people interact with the Internet. Websites are made up of individual web pages organized together and linked together. Every time you go online, you start at one web page. Navigating the Internet means that you are traveling (electronically) from one web page to another. That's why you will notice that you use "back" and "forward" buttons on your Internet browser to bring you back along the pages you have already visited.

Webmail: Webmail refers to email that you access via a web browser. Nowadays, most email accounts are accessible via a webmail interface.

Wikipedia and "Wikis": Wikipedia is one of the most commonly accessed web-sites, and it is built on a collaborative platform called a "wiki." This collaborative platform means that the website is open to be edited by anyone who signs up as a registered user; and anyone can sign up as a user.(You don't have to sign up to be a user to edit—anyone can edit.) This does not mean that the content on Wikipedia is automatically suspect: Wikipedia has an editorial process and edits are tracked and vetted.

Index

About the Author

JOEL A. NICHOLS is manages the Charles L. Durham Neighborhood Library, a branch of the Free Library of Philadelphia in Pennsylvania. He previously managed the Free Library Techmobile, a digital literacy outreach vehicle. He has also taught college English and worked as a children's librarian. Nichols holds a master of science degree in library and information science from Drexel University, a master's degree in creative writing and English from Temple University, and an bachelor's degree with honors in German from Wesleyan University. He also studied Weimar literature and history at the Humboldt-Universitaet in Berlin, Germany, supported by a Fulbright. He is author of *iPads in the Library* (Libraries Unlimited, 2013) and lives in Philadelphia with his boyfriend and their child.